AU COURANT

Everyday Expressions for Communicating in Simple French

Robert J. Johnson

National Textbook Company
a division of *NTC Publishing Group*

Published by National Textbook Company, a division of NTC Publishing Group.
©1991 by NTC Publishing Group, 4255 West Touhy Avenue,
Lincolnwood (Chicago), Illinois 60646-1975 U.S.A.
Manufactured in the United States of America.

0 1 2 3 4 5 6 7 8 9 VP 9 8 7 6 5 4 3 2 1

CONTENTS

PREFACE

Several years ago, I took a group of students to France as part of an exchange program with a French *collège* near Paris. Just before landing at Charles De Gaulle Airport, one of my braver students revealed his most secret fear: that neither he nor the others in our group would be able to communicate with their soon-to-be French friends. It seemed that the closer they were getting to the "real thing," the more trouble they were having remembering all the French they had studied.

As their French teacher, I too was a bit apprehensive. I worried that making the trip with students who had only one and a half years of French under their hats might not have been such a great idea after all. "How would it look if my students were tongue-tied!" I thought. Fortunately, there was no need to worry. Seeing each one of my students breeze through customs, and later introduce themselves to their host families, made me almost ashamed for ever having doubted them. After all, they were friendly, intelligent, open-minded, and as well prepared as could be expected. What a relief! Everyone passed the test.

Throughout our stay in France, I had ample opportunity to observe my students in action. To be frank, I was often amazed how easily they were able to manage in a language that had truly been foreign to them just a short time before. The reason for their success: they knew what to say. This may sound like an oversimplification, but many students—even after many years of study—have to struggle to say even the simplest things. Although the typical student may know a great deal of grammar and wield a more-than-adequate vocabulary, he or she usually is not familiar enough with the common, everyday expressions that tie the language together.

In preparation for the trip abroad, I provided my students with a list of 101 of the most useful expressions I could think of. I knew they needed to know certain everyday expressions ("You're welcome," "I'm sorry," "No thanks," "How much is it?," etc.) to socialize and to get in and out of shops. Unfortunately, the textbook we were using provided us with too few of these practical expressions.

Au courant is intended to equip you with the basic expressions needed to communicate in simple French. It is based on the original list of expressions, which has been both expanded and reorganized to provide you with a more powerful tool in learning to speak French. A variety of exercises and activities has been given to help you systematically master the expressions and to understand the situations in which each may be used.

Try to use the expressions in this book as often as you can. They're really very useful and easy to learn.

INTRODUCTION

▼

Au courant is a collection of basic French idioms and expressions carefully selected for their general communicative usefulness. It has been designed for beginning and intermediate students who, while attempting to master the basic idiomatic expressions of French, are simultaneously involved studying its vocabulary and structure. The text is intended, therefore, to dovetail the content of any beginning or intermediate textbook.

Students who master the expressions developed in *Au courant* will be able to communicate with much greater ease and confidence. In many cases, the expressions alone are all that is necessary to get a simple idea across. When a more detailed message is required, students can use the expressions "to buy time" needed to formulate a linguistically more complex response. In short, the deliberate use of these expressions can help to develop effective communicative strategies.

The 229 idioms and expressions that form the core of *Au courant* have been divided into three basic categories to facilitate their mastery. The categories have been given the names of colors. The *Locutions bleues* are for expressing personal feelings; the *Locutions blanches* are for getting what you need or for doing business; and the *Locutions rouges* are for socializing.

The function of these categories becomes important in Part II (*Situations*), helping direct students to the type of expression required in each situation. For example, students might be asked to find the expression needed for the following:

SITUATION   You're standing in the lunch line and your friend Marie sneezes.

YOU HEAR: Atchoum!

YOU SAY: _____
                                            Bleues #9–14?

Est-ce que tu as un mouchoir, Marie?

The student would look up the *Locutions bleues* #9 through #14 in the back of the book and decide which of the five expressions would be the best response in the situation. Of course the best answer would be <<À tes souhaits>> (or <<À vos souhaits>>). The student would then write the answer on the line provided. Note that formal and feminine forms are given in parentheses.

As in real life, there can frequently be more than one response to a given question. Any expression appropriate for the situation is acceptable as long as it is taken from the list specified, that is, *Bleues #9–14*. Therefore, expressions #9, 10, and 13 are also possible answers but #11 and #14 probably would not be acceptable. These categories are helpful in giving students direction and encouraging them to use expressions they might otherwise avoid; thus expressions such as <<Je ne sais pas>> or <<Je pense que oui>> cannot be overused.

Finally, it is strongly recommended that an effort be made to periodically review the expressions already covered. Try to use them whenever possible.

Part I

LOCUTIONS: Bleues, Blanches and Rouges

LOCUTIONS BLEUES:
Expressing Personal Feelings

LESSON ONE   **Descriptive Reactions and Responses**

1. What to Say   Expressing how you feel about people or things can often be accomplished very easily by making simple descriptions. Probably you already know many descriptive words (adjectives) that can be used to express how you feel about yourself, other people, and the things around you. Here are a few:

amusant(e)	**facile**	**joli(e)**
bon/bonne	**formidable**	**mauvais(e)**
chic	**gentil/gentille**	**sportif/sportive**
difficile	**intelligent(e)**	**sympa**
énergique	**intéressant(e)**	**triste**

Think of some good adjectives for the following, and write them in French on the lines below:

a. yourself _____

b. your teacher _____

c. your best friend _____

d. your French class _____

e. the last movie you saw _____

How did you describe the movie? Was it **bon, mauvais, intéressant,** or perhaps **triste?** No matter how you may have answered, you revealed something you thought was important about the film. Whoever reads your answer will get at least some idea how you liked it.

The French have some good expressions for putting all these descriptive words to use.

1. Comme c'est beau!	How beautiful it is!
or	
Que c'est beau!	Boy, is that ever beautiful!

Use these expressions with any descriptive adjective to show you have definite thoughts about something:

Comme c'est ridicule!	That's ridiculous!
Comme c'est triste!	How sad!
Que c'est bizarre!	How weird!
Que c'est cher!	Boy, is that ever expensive!

Here's another good expression (but not quite as definite):

2. À mon avis, c'est trop cher!	In my opinion, it's too expensive!

Like the first expressions above, this one can be used with any descriptive adjective you wish. The words **à mon avis** tend to soften your reaction.

À mon avis, c'est facile!

By the way, if you would like to learn a few more useful adjectives, here are some you can add to your list:

abominable	awful	**bizarre**	weird
actif/active	active	**calme**	calm
adorable	adorable	**capable**	capable
ambitieux/ambitieuse	ambitious	**compliqué/compliquée**	complicated
bête	dumb, stupid	**cruel/cruelle**	cruel

curieux/curieuse	curious	**marrant/marrante**	funny
distrait/distraite	absent-minded	**mignon/mignonne**	cute
dynamique	dynamic	**moche**	funny looking
égoïste	selfish	**modeste**	modest, humble
élégant/élégante	elegant	**nerveux/nerveuse**	nervous
embêtant/embêtante	annoying	**normale**	normal
émotif/émotive	emotional	**optimiste**	optimistic
énorme	enormous	**patient/patiente**	patient
enthousiaste	enthusiastic	**pessimiste**	pessimistic
fou/folle	crazy, wild	**poli/polie**	polite
généreux/généreuse	generous	**prudent/prudente**	prudent, careful
grave	serious	**rasoir**	boring
idéal/idéale	ideal	**sage**	well-behaved
indépendant/ indépendante	independent	**sale**	dirty
		sérieux/sérieuse	serious
inoubliable	unforgettable	**sévère**	strict
inutile	useless	**sincère**	sincere
irrésistible	irresistible	**sociable**	sociable
irritable	irritable	**timide**	shy
laid/laide	ugly	**utile**	useful
logique	logical		

Ask your teacher or a French-speaking friend for some others. If you don't know anyone who speaks French, you can always consult a French dictionary.

_____   _____

_____   _____

By using nouns instead of adjectives, there's another way to show how you, personally, feel about something or someone.

3. Quel dommage!	What a shame!	
	What a pity!	

Quel, or any of its forms, can be used with many nouns to show strong feeling or emotion. You can have some fun with this one.

Quelle barbe!	What a bore!	**Quel monde!**	What a crowd!
Quelle bêtise!	What nonsense!	**Quel monstre!**	What a monster!
Quelle chance!	What luck!		
Quel désastre!	What a disaster!	**Quels problèmes!**	What problems!
		Quel prof!	What a teacher!
Quel embarras!	How embarrassing!	**Quelle salade!**	What a pack of lies!
Quel ennui!	How annoying!	**Quel toupet!**	What nerve!
		Quel type!	What a character!
Quelle farce!	What a joke!		
Quel gâchis!	What a mess!		
Quelle horreur!	How horrible!		

4. Quelle bonne idée!	What a good idea!
Quelle belle musique!	What beautiful music!
Quelle jolie robe!	What a beautiful dress!
Quelle cravate abominable!	What an awful tie!

Try to think of some nouns of your own, and make sentences with **quel(le).**

_____

_____

_____

II. Application   A. Select the most appropriate expression for each of the following situations:

1.   You haven't cleaned your room in weeks. Your mother peeks in and gasps:

   a. Quelle bonne idée!

   b. Quel désastre!

   c. Comme c'est beau!

2. Your next door neighbor can't stand rock music. You have your stereo turned up much too loud, so he remarks:

   a. À mon avis, c'est parfait!

   b. Comme c'est facile!

   c. Quelle musique abominable!

3. Your little brother wants to bake a cake, but he discovers that there aren't any eggs left. He asks you if you think he should go ahead and bake it anyway. You say:

   a. À mon avis, ce n'est pas une bonne idée!

   b. À mon avis, ce n'est pas poli!

   c. Quel monde!

4. You receive a letter from your French pen pal informing you she won't be able to visit you this summer as planned. You say:

   a. Comme c'est inoubliable!

   b. Que c'est cher!

   c. Quel dommage!

5. Your friend is having trouble in math. You, on the other hand, are a whiz at math and would like to encourage him by saying:

      a. Quelle barbe!

      b. À mon avis, ce n'est pas trop compliqué!

      c. Quel prof intelligent!

B. Complete the following based on the expressions discussed in this lesson:

1. Est-ce que tu veux voir une photo de ma petite nièce? Elle a sept ans.

— Quelle belle jeune _____ !

      a. homme   c. garçon

      b. femme   d. fille

2. Mon pauvre chat est mort.

— Quel _____ !

      a. monstre   c. chance

      b. dommage   d. type

3. Le frère de David n'aime pas la glace.

— Que c'est _____ !

      a. actif   c. capable

      b. sympa   d. bizarre

4. Robert veut être président.

— Comme c'est _____ !

      a. inutile   c. moche

      b. ambitieux   d. pessimiste

5. Luc veut être président, mais il ne veut pas étudier.

— À mon avis, ce n'est pas _____ !

    a. modeste   c. logique
    b. ambitieux   d. poli

III. Amusez-vous!

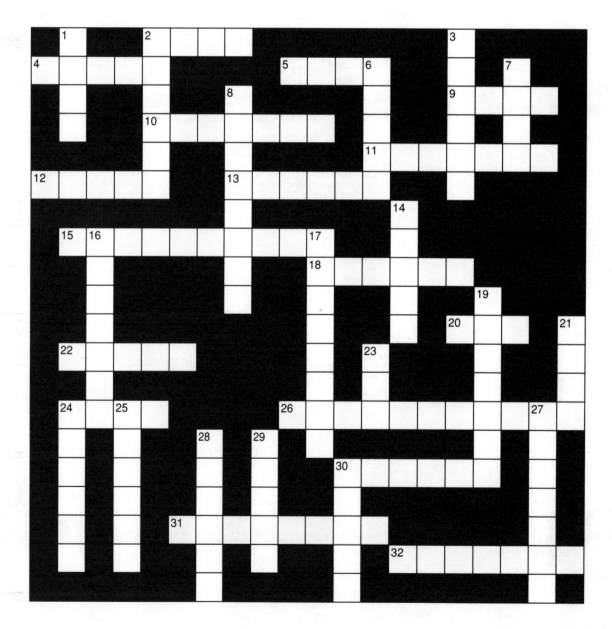

ACROSS

2. Well-behaved

4. Quel _____ ! = What a crowd!

5. Quel _____ ! = What a teacher!

9. Comme c'est _____ ! = How expensive!

10. Selfish

11. Curious

12. Useful

13. Shy

15. Quelle cravate _____ ! = What an awful tie!

18. Comme c'est _____ ! = How cute!

20. Comme c'est _____ ! = How good!

22. Serious

24. Que c'est _____ ! = How dumb!

26. Unforgettable

30. Quelle _____ ! = What luck!

31. Comme c'est _____ = How ridiculous!

32. Quel _____ ! = How horrible!

DOWN

1. Quel garçon _____ ! = What a polite boy!

2. Quel prof _____ ! = What a strict teacher!

3. Quel _____ ! = What a mess!

6. Quelle _____ ! = What a joke!

7. Comme c'est _____ ! = How beautiful!

8. Absent-minded

14. Quel _____ ! = How annoying!

16. Que c'est _____ ! = How weird!

17. Annoying, obnoxious

19. Quel _____ ! = What a shame!

21. Dirty

23. Crazy

24. Quelle _____ ! = What nonsense!

25. Comme c'est _____ = How sad!

27. Que c'est _____ ! = How logical!

28. Easy

29. Quelle _____ voiture! = What a nice car!

30. Calm

IV. Take These with You

1.	**Comme c'est beau!**	How beautiful it is!
	Que c'est beau!	Boy, is that ever beautiful!
2.	**À mon avis, c'est trop cher!**	In my opinion, it's too expensive!
3.	**Quel dommage!**	What a shame!
		What a pity!
4.	**Quelle bonne idée!**	What a good idea!

LESSON TWO   Expressing Positive Feelings: Concern, Surprise, Enthusiasm, and Joy

I. What to Say   The expressions you learned in Lesson 1 can be very useful because they enable you to react to a very wide range of situations without giving elaborate answers. However, you should also be prepared to handle situations requiring more precise responses that reveal more about how you really feel.

Lesson 2 deals with expressing more intense positive feelings like concern, surprise, enthusiasm, and joy. Since there are twenty-four expressions in this lesson, it might be a good idea to get into the habit of reviewing the expressions you have already learned.

Concern

We show concern by helping out and wishing others well when they are faced with a problem. Here's how to ask someone if something is wrong:

5.	**Qu'est-ce qui se passe?**	What's happening?
6.	**Qu'est-ce qu'il y a?**	What's the matter?
7.	**Qu'est-ce qui est arrivé?**	What happened?

If you think someone has hurt himself or herself, you might ask:

8.	**Ça te fait mal?**	Does it hurt?
	(Ça vous fait mal?)	

What is the doctor asking when he says:

Où est-ce que ça vous fait mal?

If a child or pet is hurt, you might say:

> **9. Pauvre petit(e)!**   Poor little thing!

> or

> **Pauvre Mary!**   Poor Mary!

Of course you should apologize if you are at fault by using one of the following:

> **10. J'en suis désolé(e)!**   I'm sorry!

> **11. Mille fois pardon!**   I'm awfully sorry!

What would you say if you accidentally bumped into a classmate and made him drop his books?

By the way, don't forget to show your concern when someone sneezes or coughs:

> **12. À tes souhaits!**   Bless you!
> **(À vos souhaits!)**

Surprise

One very common way to show you're surprised is to use this expression:

> **13. Oh là là!**   Wow!
>   Oh my goodness!

The French constantly use this expression and seem to have a great deal of fun with it. Sometimes, when somebody's shocked by something, the expression is lengthened to sound something like machine gun fire:

Oh là là là là là !

Here are some others:

14. **Tu parles!**   You've got to be kidding!
   (Vous parlez!)

15. **C'est trop fort!**   You're too much!

16. **Je n'en reviens pas!**   I can't get over it!

17. **Tiens, ça c'est nouveau!**   Well, that's a new one!

18. **Sans blague!**   No kidding!

19. **Ça tombe bien!**   What a coincidence!

Which of the above expressions would you choose to react to each of the following situations?

a. You have just heard a news bulletin announcing that the dam above your town has collapsed. In thirty minutes your home will be flooded.

_____

b. You have just heard that your neighbor is planning a fifty-mile bicycle trip around a nearby lake.

_____

c. Your dad informs you that you will have to help him clean out the garage this Saturday afternoon.

_____

Enthusiasm and Joy

You probably have already learned a number of important ways to show enthusiasm, such as **Bravo! Super! Formidable! Chouette! Merveilleux!** Ask your teacher or a friend for some others:

_____   _____

_____   _____

Your parents undoubtedly show their enthusiasm (or even joy) when you do well in school. Write in French on the lines below some expressions your parents might use to express how they would feel if you brought home a perfect report card:

_____

_____

_____

_____

Probably the principal of your school would also offer his congratulations:

20. Félicitations!   Congratulations!

If someone, perhaps your rich uncle, were to ask you to go with him to Paris this weekend (on the Concorde, of course), you might enthusiastically agree to accompany him by saying:

21. Et comment!   You bet!
                             And how!

Or perhaps you'd say:

22. Avec plaisir!   With pleasure!

When something very fortunate happens, you might say:

23. Grâce au ciel!   Thank heavens!

Or if you're totally ecstatic with the way things have been going, you might exclaim:

24. Il fait bon vivre!   It's great to be alive!

What would you say if you were responsible for winning a championship basketball game by sinking a half-court basket with only two seconds left in the game?

II. Application   A. Select the most appropriate expression for each of the following situations:

1. You hear a loud, banging noise coming from the garage where your dad has been working on his car. You open the door and say:

   a. Avec plaisir.

   b. Il fait bon vivre!

   c. Qu'est-ce qui se passe?

2. Your teacher is returning a test you thought you had failed. When you get your paper back, you discover that you received a B + , so you say:
    a. Ça te fait mal?
    b. Grâce au ciel!
    c. À tes souhaits!

3. Pierre, an exchange student from France who had never played baseball before, shocked everyone on your team by hitting a home run. You and your teammates show your surprise by exclaiming:
    a. J'en suis désolé(e)!
    b. Je n'en reviens pas!
    c. Mille fois pardon!

4. Your dog has been hurt, so you try to comfort him by petting him and repeating:
    a. Pauvre petit!
    b. Félicitations!
    c. Tu parles!

5. Your mother asks you if you would like to go with her to the mall to buy some new school clothes. You desperately need a few new things, so you answer:
    a. Mille fois pardon.
    b. Ça te fait mal?
    c. Et comment!

III. Amusez-vous!

Do you know another name for *le drapeau français?* To find out, complete the graph with the expressions that correspond to the English expressions below. Write your answer in the circles at the bottom of the page.

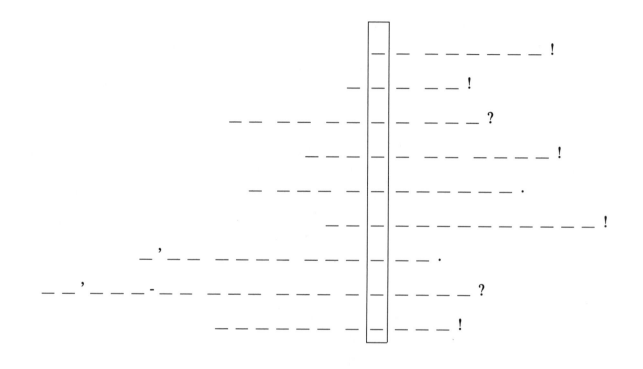

LE ◯◯◯◯◯◯◯◯◯

1. You've got to be kidding!
2. Super!
3. Does it hurt?
4. Thank heavens!
5. Bless you!

6. Congratulations!
7. I'm sorry!
8. What happened?
9. Poor little thing!

IV. Take These with You

5. **Qu'est-ce qui se passe?**	What's happening?
6. **Qu'est-ce qu'il y a?**	What's the matter?
7. **Qu'est-ce qui est arrivé?**	What happened?
8. **Ça te fait mal?** **(Ça vous fait mal?)**	Does it hurt?
9. **Pauvre petit(e)!** **Pauvre Marie!**	Poor little thing! Poor Mary!
10. **J'en suis désolé(e)!**	I'm sorry!
11. **Mille fois pardon!**	I'm awfully sorry!
12. **À tes souhaits!** **(À vos souhaits!)**	Bless you!
13. **Oh là là!**	Wow! Oh my goodness!
14. **Tu parles!** **(Vous parlez!)**	You've got to be kidding!
15. **C'est trop fort!**	You're too much!
16. **Je n'en reviens pas!**	I can't get over it!
17. **Tiens, ça c'est nouveau!**	Well, that's a new one!
18. **Sans blague!**	No kidding!
19. **Ça tombe bien!**	What a coincidence!
20. **Félicitations!**	Congratulations!
21. **Et comment!**	You bet! And how!
22. **Avec plaisir!**	With pleasure!
23. **Grâce au ciel!**	Thank heavens!
24. **Il fait bon vivre!**	It's great to be alive!

LESSON THREE   **Expressing Negative Feelings: Doubt, Impatience, Disapproval, and Anger**

The expressions you learned in Lesson 2 help you to express positive feelings for others. Sometimes, however, it is necessary to show disapproval or dismay in dealing with people.

Lesson 3 shows you how to express negative personal feelings such as doubt, impatience, disapproval, and anger. These expressions may at times sound a bit abrasive, but let's be honest, they are a fact of life and you should learn to express them in French. Besides, quite often these expressions are used jokingly among friends and need not be taken seriously.

I. What to Say   *Doubt*

Doubt includes inexactitude, which can be expressed by

25. Plus ou moins.   More or less.

—Combien d'argent as-tu?

—Dix dollars, **plus ou moins.**

A good way to suggest that you *might* do something under the right conditions is to say one of the following:

26. Peut-être.   Maybe.
                             Perhaps.

27. Ça dépend.   That depends.

28. Ça dépend de toi.   It depends on you.
     (Ça dépend de vous.)

—Est-ce que tu veux finir mes devoirs pour moi?

—**Peut-être.** Combien d'argent as-tu?

You can express more serious doubt with

29. J'en doute!   I doubt that!
                             I doubt it!

—Les Français n'aiment pas le fromage!

—J'en doute!

Which of the following would your mom most likely say if you asked her if you could spend this Friday night at your best friend's house?

a. Peut-être.

b. Ça dépend de toi.

c. J'en doute!

Impatience

Patience is a virtue we should all strive to cultivate, but sometimes it doesn't hurt to use expressions like the following:

30. Reste couvert! **(Restez couvert!)**	Keep your shirt on!
31. Décide-toi! **(Décidez-vous!)**	Make up your mind!
32. N'importe!	Never mind!

Certainly you've heard your teacher use this one just before the class bell:

33. Dépêche-toi! **(Dépêchez-vous!)**	Hurry up!

What would you probably say to a friend who spends too much time deliberating his next move when playing chess or checkers?:

a. Reste couvert!

b. Décide-toi!

c. J'en doute!

Disapproval

One way to express disapproval is to say:

34. Honte à toi!   Shame on you!
    (Honte à vous!)

Or in extreme cases, you may use one of the following:

35. J'en ai marre!   I've had it up to here!

36. Ras le bol!   I'm really fed up!

37. Je m'en fiche!   I don't give a darn!

If someone asks too many personal questions you might say:

38. Mêle-toi de tes affaires!   Mind your own business!
    (Mêlez-vous de vos
    affaires!)

If someone calls you a bad name, you might reply:

39. À toi de même!   Same to you, buddy!
    (À vous de même!)

When someone you don't like leaves the room, you could say:

40. Bon débarras!   Good riddance!

And finally, when someone does something that drives you to the end of your rope, you might say:

41. Ça, c'est le comble!   That's the last straw!
          That beats everything!

What would you say to your little brother who keeps insisting that you make him a snack, right away?

    a. Ça dépend.

    b. Reste couvert!

    c. Ça, c'est le comble!

Anger

What do you say when you are upset? In French you might simply say:

42. Ça me fait rager!		That burns me up!

or perhaps

43. Je suis furieux (furieuse)!	I'm furious!

If you're only mildly upset you might say:

44. Ça m'inquiète.	That really bugs me.

If you get upset because someone's joking has gone too far, you can say:

45. Assez de bêtises!	Enough foolishness! Knock it off!
46. Laisse-moi tranquille! (Laissez-moi tranquille!)	Leave me alone!
47. Va t'en! (Allez-vous-en!)	Get out of here! Go away!

Which of these expressions would you use if the student sitting behind you in French class kept bothering you by tapping her foot on the leg of your desk?

II. Application

A. Select the most appropriate expression for each of the following situations:

1. You and your friend Kevin are shopping for clothes. Your friend has just spent over an hour trying to decide which style shirt he should buy. You start to get a little impatient, so you say:

    a. Bon débarras!

    b. Décide-toi!

    c. À toi de même!

2. Your dad asks you how much time you spent doing your homework. You're not exactly sure, so you say:

    a. Deux heures. Je m'en fiche!

    b. Deux heures. J'en doute!

    c. Deux heures, plus ou moins.

3. An acquaintance who constantly tries to borrow money and then avoids paying it back informs you that he'll soon be moving out of town. Your *secret* reaction is:

    a. Bon débarras!

    b. Ça me fait rager!

    c. Reste couvert!

4. You just got a new haircut and it's not very flattering. Your friends have been teasing you mercilessly about it. Finally, you lose your patience and snap:

    a. Ça dépend de vous!

    b. N'importe.

    c. Assez de bêtises!

5. You are a famous French pastry maker. A competitor asks you to reveal the secret ingredient in your chocolate éclairs. Insulted she would dare ask for such a trade secret, you firmly tell her:

    a. Mêlez-vous de vos affaires!

    b. Dépêchez-vous!

    c. Décide-toi!

B. Complete the following responses based on the expressions discussed in this lesson. Choose your answers from the words in the box given below.

1. Tu es bête, David!

    —À _____ de _____ !

2. La musique américaine n'est pas populaire en France.

    —J'en _____ .

3. Combien d'argent avez-vous, Monsieur?

    —Mêlez- _____ de vos _____ !

4. Dépêche-toi, Chantal! Nous sommes en retard!

    — _____ couvert!

5. Oh là là! Je n'ai pas étudié le français hier soir!

    — _____ à toi!

doute	Honte
Reste	toi
vous	affaires
même	

III. Take These with You

25.	Plus ou moins.	More or less.
26.	Peut-être.	Maybe. Perhaps.
27.	Ça dépend.	That depends.
28.	Ça dépend de toi. Ça dépend de vous.	That depends on you.
29.	J'en doute!	I doubt that! I doubt it!
30.	Reste couvert! (Restez couvert!)	Keep your shirt on!
31.	Décide-toi! (Décidez-vous!)	Make up your mind!
32.	N'importe!	Never mind!
33.	Dépêche-toi! (Dépêchez-vous!)	Hurry up!
34.	Honte à toi! (Honte à vous!)	Shame on you!
35.	J'en ai marre!	I've had it up to here!
36.	Ras le bol!	I'm really fed up!
37.	Je m'en fiche!	I don't give a darn!
38.	Mêle-toi de tes affaires! (Mêlez-vous de vos affaires!)	Mind your own business!
39.	À toi de même! (À vous de même!)	Same to you, buddy!
40.	Bon débarras!	Good riddance!

41. Ça, c'est le comble!	That's the last straw! That beats everything!
42. Ça me fait rager!	That burns me up!
43. Je suis furieux (furieuse)!	I'm furious!
44. Ça m'inquiète!	That really bugs me!
45. Assez de bêtises!	Enough foolishness! Knock it off!
46. Laisse-moi tranquille! (Laissez-moi tranquille!)	Leave me alone!
47. Va t'en! (Allez-vous-en!)	Get out of here! Go away!

LOCUTIONS BLANCHES:
Getting What You Need

LESSON FOUR   **Expressing Confusion and Lack of Understanding**

The first three lessons of this book *(Locutions bleues)* dealt with communicating personal feelings. The *Locutions blanches,* which you will study in the next six lessons, will help you to deal with French-speaking people when you need to get information or conduct business. Before attempting either of these in French, perhaps the first thing you should do is learn what to say when you don't understand what is being said or when you need a slower or simpler explanation.

I. What to Say   Let's be honest. As a beginner, there will be many times when you will become confused or simply won't be able to understand what native speakers are saying in French. It is important, then, that you learn to politely ask for clarification in order to get yourself back on track.

You never want to buy anything without completely knowing the terms of a sale, so it's important to get others to explain what they mean when you are conducting business. Don't be afraid to ask the clerk how much something costs or to ask for an explanation of any other conditions of the sale.

Certainly, when talking to a friend, you should feel free to explain that you have misunderstood something and that you need your friend's help in understanding it. Just be certain to do so politely.

There are three things you should do when you're confused or don't understand something: A. politely interrupt the speaker, B. inform the speaker that you don't understand, C. ask the speaker to repeat or re-explain what you don't understand.

Let's zero in on each of these:

A. *Politely Interrupt the Speaker.*

Any way of saying "Please," "I'm sorry," or "Excuse me" will accomplish this. You already know *Bleues #10*:

J'en suis désolé(e).   I'm sorry.

Here are two ways to say "Please":

1. Je t'en prie.
**   (Je vous en prie.)**
                              Please.
2. S'il vous plaît.

And here is how to say "Excuse me."

3. Excuse-moi.
**   (Excusez-moi.)**
                              Excuse me.
4. Je m'excuse.

5. Pardon.
                              Pardon me.
6. Pardonne-moi.
**   (Pardonnez-moi.)**

Of course you can put "Please" and "Excuse me" together for a very polite effect:

Excusez-moi, s'il vous plaît.

B. *Inform the Speaker that You Don't Understand.*

This is best accomplished by stating one of the following:

7. Je ne comprends pas.   I don't understand.

8. Je n'ai pas compris.   I didn't understand.

9. Je ne t'ai pas entendu.   I didn't hear you.
**   (Je ne vous ai pas**
**   entendu.)**

C. Ask the Speaker to Repeat or Re-explain What You Don't Understand.

10. Encore une fois.	Again. One more time.
11. Répète. **(Répétez.)**	Repeat.
12. Parle plus lentement. **(Parlez plus lentement.)**	Speak more slowly.
or you can ask:	
13. Est-ce que tu as dit X ou Y? **(Est-ce que vous avez dit X ou Y?)**	Did you say X or Y?

For example, imagine you are in Martinique and you'd like to buy a certain souvenir for your favorite uncle. You ask the clerk how much it costs, but you don't quite understand if she said 14 F or 40 F, so you say:

Pardonnez-moi Mademoiselle. **Est-ce que vous avez dit** 14 francs ou 40 francs? **Je ne vous ai pas entendue.**

Sometimes, especially with friends, it's appropriate to say:

14. Qu'est-ce que tu as dit? **(Qu'est-ce que vous avez dit?)**	What did you say?

By the way, you should know that people have a natural tendency to speak more slowly and clearly when they realize you are just learning their language. Make this work for you by reminding native speakers that French is not your native language. Since your accent will easily give you away, you can best accomplish this by asking lots of questions and by talking as much as you can. If, for example, you are with three or four French friends and you find that they are speaking much too fast for you, slow them down by saying something. It will force them to tailor the conversation to your level of understanding. The more involved in the conversation you become, the slower they will speak and the more you will be able to understand.

II. Application

A. Imagine that you are riding home on the bus listening to Jim relate what Jackie said about you at lunch. There is so much noise on the bus that you can't hear the best part. Write in French what you would say to get Jim to repeat what you missed. (Don't forget the three steps discussed on pages 26–28).

1. _____

2. _____

3. _____

B. Imagine that you are eating pizza with a small group of French foreign exchange students who have been studying at your school for about a month. Since you are the only nonnative speaker of French in their company, your friends decide it would be easier to talk in French. Before you realize it, they're speaking so fast that you can barely understand what they're talking about. (By the way, they're talking about how much they enjoyed the American movie they saw last Friday night.) Which of the following expressions can you use to politely slow them down so you can get back into the conversation? Write your answers on the lines provided below:

Moi aussi, j'adore la cuisine chinoise.
Parlez plus lentement, je vous en prie.

À vos souhaits!

Excusez-moi, mais je ne comprends pas.

Ça vous fait mal?

J'en ai marre!

Encore une fois; je n'ai pas compris.

Bon débarras!

Répétez, s'il vous plaît. Je ne vous ai pas entendu.

À vous de même!

Write your answers here:

1. _____

2. _____

3. _____

4. _____

Do you think your French teacher would like you to use these expressions in class when there's something you don't understand?

III. Situations

Although it isn't polite, bilingual people who don't realize you speak their language sometimes intentionally use their native language to keep you from understanding what they're saying. Pretend you overhear some people talking about you in French. Decide which of the four responses given below would work best in making them aware that you can understand the conversation.

1. SITUATION: You're a businessman taking the subway to work and you overhear a little boy tell his mother in French how funny he thinks your necktie looks.

YOU HEAR: **Maman, cet homme-là porte une cravate comme le pyjama de papa!**

YOU SAY: _____

2. SITUATION: You're a young woman in a department store elevator. You overhear someone else in the elevator criticize your perfume.

YOU HEAR: **Quelle odeur! Le parfum de la demoiselle est abominable!**

YOU SAY: _____

3. SITUATION: You're the owner of a restaurant in Buffalo, New York. You happen to notice two French gentlemen leaving your restaurant complaining about the service.

YOU HEAR: **Quel restaurant! Et quel garçon impoli!**

YOU SAY: _____

4. SITUATION: You're a teenage boy in a café and you overhear two French girls talking about you.

YOU HEAR: **Yvette, regarde ce garçon-là! Comme il est beau, n'est-ce pas?**

YOU SAY: _____

Choice of Responses   <<Qu'est-ce que tu as dit? Tu voudrais une cravate comme celle-ci pour Noël!>>

<<Excusez-moi, messieurs. Je suis le propriétaire. Est-ce qu'il y a un problème?>>

<<Pardonnez-moi, s'il vous plaît. Savez-vous à quel étage se trouve le rayon des chaussures?>>

<<Pardonnez-moi, mais est-ce que vous avez dit que vous aimez mon chapeau?>>

This time your response is given, but you make up the situation:

5. SITUATION: _____

_____

_____

YOU HEAR: _____

_____

_____

YOU SAY: <<Tu parles! Tu n'aimes pas la chanson que j'ai écrite!>>

IV. Take These with You

1. **Je t'en prie.**
   (Je vous en prie.)

   Please.

2. **S'il vous plaît.**

3. **Excuse-moi**
   (Excusez-moi.)

   Excuse me.

4. **Je m'excuse.**

5. **Pardon.**

   Pardon me.

6. **Pardonne-moi.**
   (Pardonnez-moi.)

7. **Je ne comprends pas.**   I don't understand.

8. **Je n'ai pas compris.**   I didn't understand.

9. **Je ne t'ai pas entendu,**   I didn't hear you.
   (Je ne vous ai pas
   entendu.)

10. **Encore une fois.**   Again.
    One more time.

11. **Répète.**   Repeat.
    (Répétez.)

12. **Parle plus lentement.**   Speak more slowly.
    (Parlez plus lentement.)

13. **Est-ce que tu as dit X**   Did you say X or Y?
    ou Y?
    (Est-ce que vous avez
    dit X ou Y?)

14. **Qu'est-ce que tu as dit?**   What did you say?
    (Qu'est-ce que vous
    avez dit?)

LESSON FIVE   **Expressing Needs, Desires, and Obligations**

Locutions Blanches are meant to help you get the information and things you need in everyday life. In this lesson you will learn what to say when you need or want something. The expressions you will learn can also be used to state obligations you must fulfill. Because you can use these expressions in a wide variety of situations, you should master them thoroughly. Learning them won't be difficult; you need only a handful to express your needs, desires, and obligations.

I. What to Say   Let's say you're taking a shower and you discover that you don't have a towel. You're sure that your little brother wouldn't mind getting you one, so you shout:

15. **J'ai besoin d'***une serviette!*

       or   *I need a* towel!

16. **Il me faut** *une serviette!*

Your brother probably won't get you a towel because you didn't say **s'il vous plaît.** Remember, whenever asking for something...

17. **Il faut dire <<S'il vous plaît>>.**   *You must say* "Please."

Il faut... is used to talk about things that you have to do. It is frequently used by parents and teachers for laying down the rules. Here are some examples:

Il faut étudier.	*You have to* study.
Il faut finir les légumes.	*You must* finish your vegetables.
Il faut lever la main si vous avez une question.	*You must* raise your hand if you have a question.
Il faut faire attention en classe.	*You have to* pay attention in class

Because **Il faut**... is an impersonal expression, it can be translated in a variety of ways. For example, **Il faut être à l'heure** can mean any of the following:

You must be on time.	We have to be on time.
One must be on time.	People have to be on time.
You have to be on time.	Etc.
I have to be on time.	

It might be a good idea to think of **Il faut**... as meaning *It is necessary*.... Usually you can determine the best equivalent of **Il faut** ...by the way it is used in a particular situation. Consider the following:

Robert is usually late for class. His teacher must constantly reprimand him for his tardiness:

—Robert, il est déjà 9h 15! **Il faut** arriver à l'heure, n'est-ce pas?

In this situation, we can easily see that it is Robert, not the teacher, who must try to get to class on time.

There is another, milder way to express obligation:

18. On doit...   One should...

This is a great expression for giving advice. Here are some examples:

On doit être prudent.	*One should* be careful.
On doit se coucher tôt.	*You should* go to bed early.
On doit se brosser les dents après les repas.	*You should* brush your teeth after meals.
On ne doit pas dormir en classe.	*One shouldn't* sleep in class.

Now imagine that you are a teacher who, on the first day of school, is explaining the class rules to a new group of students. List your three most important rules below:

1. Il faut _____

2. Il faut _____

3. Il ne faut pas _____

Also give your students some friendly advice to help them have a more productive experience.

1. On doit _____

2. On doit _____

3. On ne doit pas _____

Perhaps the best expression for stating what you need is:

19. Je voudrais...   I would like...

Here are some examples:

Je voudrais une voiture de sport rouge.

Je voudrais des amis qui me comprennent.

Je voudrais aller au cinéma ce soir.

Je voudrais faire un voyage en France.

Pretend that you have just been granted three wishes by a genie. Write your list of wishes on the lines below:

1. Je voudrais _____

2. Je voudrais _____

3. Je voudrais _____

II. Application

A. Choose the most appropriate expression for each of the following situations:

1. You are taking an important examination and you break your pencil. You need another, so you raise your hand and politely say:

   a. Il faut avoir un crayon.

   b. J'ai besoin d'un autre crayon, s'il vous plaît.

   c. On doit finir l'examen, n'est-ce pas?

2. Your mother is an English teacher who simply cannot tolerate poor grammar. Your French friend, Yvette, who is visiting for two weeks, has picked up the term *ain't* from another friend. Afraid your mom might be upset, you warn Yvette:

   a. Il me faut un dictionnaire, Yvette!

   b. Il ne faut pas parler anglais, Yvette.

   c. On ne doit pas dire <<ain't>>, Yvette.

3. You're a high-school track coach, and you're trying to get your team in shape. Which advice would you *not* give your athletes?

   a. On doit courir plus vite!

   b. On doit trop manger!

   c. On doit faire ses exercises!

4. You're lost in the desert, and you haven't had a drink of water in days. Which of the following would you be least likely to find yourself repeating while wandering through the desert?

    a. J'ai besoin d'eau.

    b. Il me faut quelque chose à boire.

    c. J'ai besoin de manger du sable.

5. You're at home by yourself after midnight, and you think you hear someone trying to break into the house. What do you think you should do?

    a. On doit téléphoner tout de suite à la police.

    b. On doit se cacher au-dessous de la couverture.

    c. On doit préparer quelque chose à manger.

B. Imagine that you are sixteen years old and that you live in a country ruled by teenagers. You have been selected to serve on a committee that sets up the rules that teachers and parents must obey. List three new rules for each. Here are some examples:

For teachers: Il ne faut pas donner des devoirs trop difficiles.

For parents: Il faut toujours écouter le rock à la radio.

Now make some up on your own:

For teachers:

1. _____

_____

2. _____

_____

3. _____

_____

For parents:

1. _____

_____

2. _____

_____

3. _____

_____

III. Amusez-vous!   In Lesson 4, you learned ways to cope with the native speaker's rapid speech. When you can't understand people because they're speaking too fast, you can ask them to repeat what they said or you can get them to slow down. But what do you do when *they* can't understand *you?* A simple solution is to use pantomime.

Here's an activity that gets you to communicate your needs when you don't know what something is called in French or when the person you're talking to can't understand what you are asking for.

Using combinations of language (*Blanches #15–19*) and pantomime, show how you would express each of the following:

1. Quick…I need a fire extinguisher!

2. For dinner, I'd like to try frogs' legs.

3. Stop that! You shouldn't chew your fingernails.

4. I have a terrible headache. I think I have to lie down.

5. Excuse me, please. I have to buy fish food and I can't seem to find it.

Now try making up some of your own.

IV. Take These
with You

15. **J'ai besoin d'une**
 serviette!

         I need a towel!

16. **Il me faut une**
 serviette!

17. **Il faut dire <<S'il vous** You must say "Please."
 plaît.>>

18. **On doit...**   One should...

19. **Je voudrais...**   I would like...

LESSON SIX **Going Shopping**

Walking into a store and making a purchase is one of the most important survival skills. Most purchases require a minimal use of the language because the price of most items is usually clearly marked. If you do have to ask how much something costs, it will be easy with the expressions you will learn in this lesson. Don't forget to always be polite when making a purchase. (**Merci** and **S'il vous plaît** will do nicely.) Finally, don't forget to review your numbers, just to be certain that you can understand how much things cost and how much change you should receive.

I. What to Say Upon entering a store, it's very likely that someone will ask you one of the following questions:

20. **Est-ce que je peux vous**
 aider?

    or   May I help you?

21. **Vous désirez?**

Perhaps you're not seriously interested in buying anything, so you reply:

22. Merci, je regarde.   No thanks, I'm only looking.

If you do want to buy something, you can use *Blanches #19:* **Je voudrais. . . .** For example:

Je voudrais voir vos voitures de sport rouges, s'il vous plaît.

How would you ask to see each of the following?

Pink sneakers _____

_____

A diamond ring _____

_____

Roller skates _____

_____

Sometimes when you're shopping (especially when you're shopping for clothes), you might have some trouble deciding what to buy. Let's say, for example, that you're shopping with a friend, and two T-shirts catch your eye. You can't decide if you would rather buy the red T-shirt or the blue one. Your friend might try to get you to hurry up by saying:

Bleues #31: **Décide-toi!**   Make up your mind!

You might answer:

Bleues #30: **Reste couvert!**   Keep your shirt on!

Then your friend might ask:

23. Lequel (Laquelle) est-ce que tu préfères?   Which one do you like better?

You can give in to your friend's impatience by saying:

24. Ni l'un(e) ni l'autre.   Neither one.

Or you might try flipping a coin:

25. Pile ou face.   Heads or tails.
(Really, tails or heads)

If your friend is genuinely trying to be helpful, he or she might make a suggestion:

26. Je préfère *le bleu foncé.*   *I prefer* the dark blue one.

Of course, you might like to try the T-shirt on, so ask:

27. Est-ce que je peux   May I try it on?
l'essayer?

If you're still having trouble making up your mind, ask your friend for his or her opinion:

28. Comment le trouves-tu?   How do you like it?
(Comment le
trouvez-vous?)

Your friend might respond in a variety of ways, like

Pouah! Comme c'est abominable!!!

It's more likely that you'll hear either:

29. Ça me plaît.   I like it.
or
30. Ça ne me plaît pas.   I don't like it.

By now you have probably made up your mind. If you want to buy it, you can ask:

31. Ça coûte combien?   How much does this cost?

By the way, you already know a good expression for complaining about the price:

Bleues #2: **À mon avis, c'est trop cher!**   In my opinion, it's too expensive!

This expression can be useful for giving other reasons for not buying something:

C'est trop grand!   It's too big!

C'est trop petit!   It's too little!

C'est trop serré!   It's too tight!

C'est trop moche!   It's too ugly!

Finally, after you have made up your mind, you can tell the clerk:

Blanches #19: **Je voudrais acheter** le tee-shirt rouge.   *I'd like to buy* the red T-shirt.

or you can say:

32. Je le prends. (Je la prends.)   I'll take it.

Before you pay for the T-shirt, the clerk will ask:

33. Est-ce tout?   Will that be all?

When you go to pay, the cashier will ask:

34. Comptant ou carte de crédit?   Cash or charge?

The cashier will no doubt thank you for making the purchase. In this situation, it would be best for you to respond by saying:

35. Il n'y a pas de quoi.   You're welcome.

II. Application   A. Select the most appropriate expression for each of the following situations:

1. There are some nice souvenir shops near Notre Dame Cathedral in Paris. You have something special in mind for your best friend back home, so you plan to browse through a number of these shops before making up your mind. Upon entering the very first shop, you are greeted by a clerk who inquires, <<Vous désirez?>> You respond:

    a. Il n'y a pas de quoi.

    b. Est-ce que je peux vous aider?

    c. Merci, je regarde.

2. You're in a pet shop looking for goldfish. There are so many kinds of exotic tropical fish that you are unable to find the goldfish, so you decide to ask the clerk for help by saying:

    a. Pardonnez-moi, je voudrais acheter des poissons rouges, mais je ne peux pas les trouver.

    b. Pile ou face?

    c. Lequel est-ce que tu préfères?

3. After making a purchase in a record store, the clerk thanks you while handing you your change and package. You respond by saying:

    a. Ça dépend, Mademoiselle.

    b. Il n'y a pas de quoi. Au revoir, Madame.

    c. Reste couvert, Monsieur.

4. You and your family are spending your vacation at the beach this summer. While unpacking your bags at the hotel, you discover that you have forgotten your bathing suit. Your only choice is to buy a new one. You and your mom go to a nearby shop, but the only two suits they have in stock are really too old-fashioned. When the clerk asks, <<Lequel est-ce que tu préfères?>> You say:

    a. C'est trop chic!

    b. Ni l'un ni l'autre!

    c. Décide-toi!

5. In another store, you are lucky to find a variety of great-looking bathing suits. The first one you try on doesn't fit. You say:

    a. À mon avis, c'est trop serré!

    b. À mon avis, c'est trop cher!

    c. À mon avis, c'est beaucoup trop moche!

B. Complete the following based on the expressions discussed in this chapter. Choose your answers from the words given in the box:

1. Est-ce que je peux vous _____ ?

    —Oui, merci. Je voudrais acheter une nouvelle voiture de sport rouge.

2. Merci beaucoup, Madame.

    —Il n'y a pas de _____ .

3. Laquelle est-ce que tu _____ ?

    —Ni l'une ni l'autre.

4. Voulez-vous payer _____ ou avec une carte de crédit, Monsieur?

    —Avec une carte de crédit, s'il vous plaît.

5. Cette cassette coûte vingt-cinq dollars.

—Oh là là! C'est beaucoup trop _____ !

comptant   quoi   cher   aider   préfères

III. Take These with You

20. Est-ce que je peux vous aider?		
21. Vous désirez?	May I help you?	
22. Merci, je regarde.	No thanks, I'm only looking.	
23. Lequel (Laquelle) est-ce que tu préfères? (Lequel [Laquelle] est-ce que vous préférez?)	Which one do you like better?	
24. Ni l'un(e) ni l'autre.	Neither one.	
25. Pile ou face.	Heads or tails.	
26. Je préfère le bleu foncé.	I prefer the dark blue one.	
27. Est-ce que je peux l'essayer?	May I try it on?	
28. Comment le trouves-tu? (Comment le trouvez-vous?)	How do you like it?	
29. Ça me plaît.	I like it.	
30. Ça ne me plaît pas.	I don't like it.	
31. Ça coûte combien?	How much does this cost?	
32. Je le prends. (Je la prends.)	I'll take it.	

33. **Est-ce tout?**	Will that be all?
34. **Comptant ou carte de crédit?**	Cash or charge?
35. **Il n'y a pas de quoi.**	You're welcome.

LESSON SEVEN   Food and Drink

You have probably already learned the basic vocabulary for food and drink, and you probably know something about French cuisine. Ordering food in a restaurant, or buying food in a store, is simply a matter of combining the food vocabulary you already know with the shopping expressions you learned in Lesson 6. For example, if you were to go to a hockey game in Montreal (perhaps to see the Montreal Canadiens play hockey at the Forum), you would probably find yourself attempting to buy something to eat at one of the concession stands. The conversation with the vendor would probably go something like this:

VENDEUR: Vous désirez?

VOUS: Je voudrais un hamburger, des frites et du Pepsi, s'il vous plaît.

VENDEUR: Est-ce tout?

VOUS: Oui, c'est tout. Et ça coûte combien?

VENDEUR: Ça coûte cinq dollars cinquante. Merci.

VOUS: Il n'y a pas de quoi.

Of course, ordering food will not always be this easy. Nevertheless, you'll do just fine, even at very exclusive French restaurants, if you have mastered the expressions *Blanches #20–35*.

In Lesson 7, you'll learn some new expressions for ordering food in restaurants. You'll also learn a few expressions for buying groceries at the outdoor market or in specialty shops. Finally, you'll learn some basic expressions commonly used at the table when dining with family or friends.

I. What to Say

At the Restaurant

Upon entering a restaurant, the maître d'hôtel will ask you: **Une table pour combien de personnes?** Your answer is simply:

36. Une table pour deux personnes, s'il vous plaît.   A table for two, please.

If you'd like an outdoor table, you can add:

37. Sur la terrasse, s'il vous plaît.   On the terrace, please.

Once seated, you'll be asked if you would like something to drink:

38. Désirez-vous un apéritif?   Would you like a before-dinner drink?

Once again, you can answer with either *Blanches #19:*

Je voudrais de l'eau minérale, s'il vous plaît.   I'd like some mineral water, please.

or

39. Rien pour moi, merci.   Nothing for me, thanks.

When ordering food or drink, you might prefer to use the following expression instead of **Je voudrais...:**

40. Je prendrai...   I'll have...

For example, if ordering French onion soup, you might say:

Je prendrai de la soupe à l'oignon, s'il vous plaît.

Using your dictionary, write what you would say to order each of the following:

Roast chicken _____

Potatoes _____

Green beans _____

A piece of chocolate cake _____

When ordering steak, it is helpful to be familiar with the following expressions:

41. Bien cuit	Well done
42. À point	Medium
43. Saignant	Rare

For example:

Je prendrai un bifteck **bien cuit.**

If you can't decide what to order, don't flip a coin. Instead ask the waiter:

44. Qu'est-ce que vous recommandez?	What do you recommend?

The waiter will probably recommend the specialty of the day **(le plat du jour).**

If you need more time to decide, you can use *Blanches #16:*

Il me faut un moment, s'il vous plaît.

When you have finished ordering, you can say:

45. Je suis servi(e), merci.	That will be all, thanks.

And when you need the check, discretely inform the waiter by saying:

46. Garçon, l'addition, s'il vous plaît.	Waiter, the check please.

The Outdoor Market and Shops

Where would you go if you had to buy food for a picnic? In many parts of France, the supermarket would probably be the most convenient place. Most French people, however, generally prefer to go elsewhere for their food. Bread, fruit, vegetables, and the like can be purchased fresh at both the outdoor market and the grocery store. In fact, the French enjoy a wide variety of shops where quality is more important than convenience. Here are some examples:

la boulangerie	the bakery
la boucherie	the butcher shop
la laiterie	the dairy
la charcuterie	the delicatessen
l'épicerie	the grocery store
le marchand de poissons	the fish store

Buying food at one of these shops or the outdoor market is much different from buying at the supermarket because there is considerably more interaction between the vendor and the customer. At the supermarket, each item has a fixed price, and of course, you serve yourself. In shops and at the outdoor market, the vendor will often try to entice you to buy his product either by lowering the price or by reminding you how fresh the item is.

In order to buy food at the outdoor market, you must learn how to express how food is sold. Although the quantities and types of food may vary, the expressions remain the same. For example, a vendor selling strawberries might say:

Madame, j'ai de belles fraises pour vous aujourd'hui! **Douze francs le kilo!** Regardez Madame!

47. Douze francs le kilo!   Twelve francs a kilo!

It would be helpful for you to familiarize yourself with some of the other ways food can be sold:

How Food Is Sold	Example
By the bottle	L'eau minérale, 9 F 50 la bouteille
can or box	Les fèves, 10 F la boîte
bag	Les bonbons, 15 F 85 le paquet
dozen	Les beignets, 20 F la douzaine
gram	300 g de fromage, 6 F les 100 g
kilo	Les fraises, 12 F le kilo
pound	Les tomates, 8 F 25
Apiece	Les melons, 11 F la pièce

At the outdoor market you can buy other things too:

By the pair   **Les chaussettes, 10 F la paire**

By the meter   **Le tissu, 5 F le mètre**

How do you think the following items would be priced? Fill in the blanks below:

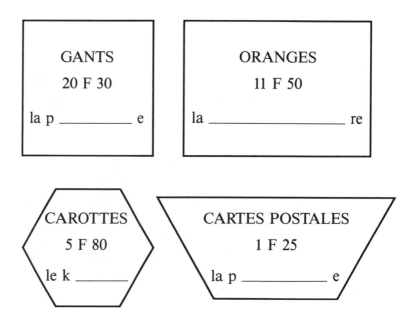

GANTS

20 F 30

la p _____ e

ORANGES

11 F 50

la _____ re

CAROTTES

5 F 80

le k _____

CARTES POSTALES

1 F 25

la p _____ e

At the Dinner Table

Now that you have a pretty good idea what to expect at the market, let's work on what to say at the dinner table.

Of course the first thing you should be able to say is that you're hungry and thirsty:

48 J'ai faim.	I'm hungry.
49. J'ai soif.	I'm thirsty.

If you're very hungry or thirsty, you can say:

50. Je meurs de faim.	I'm dying of hunger.
51. Je meurs de soif.	I'm dying of thirst.

If you're absolutely famished you might say:

52. J'ai une faim de loup!	I'm so hungry I could eat a horse! (literally: I'm as hungry as a wolf.)

When dinner is ready you will hear:

53. À table!	Time to eat!

Before eating, someone will probably say:

54. Bon appétit!	Eat hearty! Enjoy!

After being seated, you might be invited to serve yourself.

55. Sers-toi! (**Servez-vous!**)	Help yourself!

Remember never to be rude when you don't like what's on the table. Use this expression only when joking:

56. Pouah!   Yuk!

When the host or hostess suggests you eat something you don't particularly care for, accept it graciously or simply ask for a small portion:

57. Un peu   A little bit

58. Un petit peu   A very little bit

If you're being served too large a portion, you can say:

59. Ça suffit!   That's enough!

(But don't forget to add **Merci.**)

Finally, you should praise your host or hostess by using *Bleues #1* with an appropriate adjective:

Comme c'est délicieux!

Here's another popular expression used to show how good you think something tastes:

60. C'est si bon!   This is really good!

II. Application   A. You and some friends are dining at the Tour d'Argent, one of
the most celebrated restaurants of Paris. Below is a scrambled
list of expressions taken from your friend Joan's conversation
with a waiter. For each expression, identify the person talking:

1. **Rien pour moi, merci.**   Joan

2. **Désirez-vous un apéritif?**   Garçon

3. **Une table pour combien de personnes?**   _____

4. **Je prendrai le canard à l'orange, s'il
    vous plaît.**   _____

5. **Est-ce tout?**   _____

6. **Je préfère le vin blanc.**   _____

7. **Comme c'est délicieux!**   _____

8. **Comment trouvez-vous le potage, Made-
    moiselle?**   _____

9. **Qu'est-ce que vous recommandez?**   _____

10. **Je suis servie, merci.**   _____

B. Look over the following grocery list. Calculate how much money you would have to spend for each item, then figure out the amount of money needed to pay the bill:

Liste de provisions

3 bouteilles d'eau minérale/9 F 50 la bouteille	=	_____
4 boîtes de fèves/15 F 45 la boîte	=	_____
1 paquet de bonbons/3 F 85 le paquet	=	_____
1 pastèque/10 F la pièce	=	_____
2 douzaines d'œufs/11 F 25 la douzaine	=	_____
600 g de fromage/12 F les 200 g	=	_____
2 livres de poires/9 F 75 la livre	=	_____
2 kilos de cerises/10 F 25 le kg	=	_____
TOTAL	=	_____

Now figure out how much change the cashier should give you if you give her 250 francs to cover the bill.

CHANGE   =   _____

C. Select the most appropriate expression for each of the following situations:

1. Your mother has prepared a *salade niçoise* for the very first time. (A *salade niçoise* is a delicious salad specialty of Nice, made of various local ingredients and topped with anchovies.) Although you're not very fond of anchovies, you don't want to hurt your mother's feelings when she asks if you would like seconds, so you say:

   a. Je voudrais un hamburger et des frites, Maman!
   b. Oui, un petit peu. Merci Maman.
   c. Pouah! Moi, je déteste les anchois!

2. Your sister Jessica has just poured herself a bowl of cereal and asks you if you would like some too. You say yes. Unfortunately, Jessica is not paying attention to what she's doing and begins pouring too much cereal into your bowl. Excitedly, you say:

    a. J'ai une faim de loup!

    b. Jessica, je n'ai pas soif!

    c. Ça suffit! Ça suffit!

3. You recently had *escargots* (snails) at a French Club meeting and were surprised that you liked them. Eager to share this new experience with your family, you go to the gourmet section of your supermarket and buy a can of *escargots* to prepare for dinner. As you place the steaming casserole on the table, you invite everyone to sit down by saying:

    a. À table, tout le monde! Bon appétit!

    b. Comme c'est chaud!

    c. Les escargots coûtent 25 F 80 la boîte!

4. Your older sister Carrie was the one who enjoyed the escargots the most. This was apparent because you heard her remark:

    a. Pouah!

    b. Ça suffit!

    c. C'est si bon!

5. You're at the outdoor market, and you would like to buy some bananas. The vendor tells you how much they're selling for today *(11 F 25 la livre)*. Since your budget will not allow you to spend more than 35 francs for bananas, what will you tell the vendor when making your purchase?

    a. Je voudrais deux livres de bananes, s'il vous plaît.

    b. Je voudrais trois livres de bananes, s'il vous plaît.

    c. Je voudrais quatre livres de bananes, s'il vous plaît.

III. Amusez-vous

A. Bon Appetit!

Here's how to make a great *salade niçoise.* Try it. It's easy!

Prepare the *vinaigrette,* or salad dressing.

In a small bowl, mix

1 cup salad oil

¹/₃ cup vinegar

1 teaspoon sugar

¹/₂ teaspoon salt

dash of garlic powder

Prepare the salad. In a large salad bowl, separate the leaves of one head of lettuce. Top with the following:

2 large tomatoes, cut in wedges

1 cucumber, sliced

1 small onion, thinly sliced

¹/₂ cup chopped celery

¹/₂ cup chopped green pepper

¹/₂ cup pitted black olives

anchovies, tuna, or sardines

Pour the *vinaigrette* over the salade and serve.

B. Here's a famous tongue-twister you'll want to learn:

COMBIEN SONT CES SAUCISSONS-CI?
CES SAUCISSONS-CI SONT SIX SOUS.

(Translation: How much are these sausages?
These sausages are six cents.)

IV. Take These with You

36. **Une table pour deux personnes, s'il vous plaît.**

A table for two, please.

37. **Sur la terrasse, s'il vous plaît.**

On the terrasse, please.

38. Désirez-vous un apéritif?	Would you like a before-dinner drink?
39. Rien pour moi, merci.	Nothing for me, thanks.
40. Je prendrai...	I'll have...
41. Bien cuit	Well done
42. À point	Medium
43. Saignant	Rare
44. Qu'est-ce que vous recommandez?	What do you recommend?
45. Je suis servi(e), merci.	That will be all, thanks.
46. Garçon, l'addition, s'il vous plaît.	Waiter, the check please.
47. Douze francs le kilo!	Twelve francs a kilo!
48. J'ai faim.	I'm hungry.
49. J'ai soif.	I'm thirsty.
50. Je meurs de faim.	I'm dying of hunger.
51. Je meurs de soif.	I'm dying of thirst.
52. J'ai une faim de loup!	I'm so hungry I could eat a horse! (literally: I'm as hungry as a wolf.)
53. À table!	Time to eat!
54. Bon appétit!	Eat hearty! Enjoy!
55. Sers-toi! (Servez-vous!)	Help yourself!
56. Pouah!	Yuk!

57. Un peu	A little bit
58. Un petit peu	A very little bit
59. Ça suffit!	That's enough!
60. C'est si bon!	This is really good!

LESSON EIGHT   Giving and Understanding Directions

Knowing how to give and understand directions is an extremely important survival skill. Without it you could easily ruin a trip abroad for yourself or others.

Before leaving, be certain to study carefully whatever maps and information you can find on the area you plan to visit. A mental image of the place you're visiting will help you to avoid getting lost and to better understand directions. Of course, the best thing you can do to avoid getting lost is to study the expressions that follow in Lesson 8.

I. What to Say

Let's begin with

61. Je me suis perdu (perdue).	I'm lost.

Let's hope you'll never have to tell anyone that you're lost because you'll always be able to ask how to get to your destination. Here are three good ways of asking:

62. Peux-tu me dire comment aller à l'hôpital? (Pouvez-vous me dire comment aller à l'hôpital?)	Can you tell me how to get to the hospital?

63. Est-ce que l'hôpital est près d'ici?	Is the hospital nearby?
64. Où se trouve l'hôpital?	Where is the hospital?

Here is a variety of expressions that you can use in different combinations to answer the three basic questions above:

65. C'est loin d'ici.	It's far away.
66. C'est tout près.	It's nearby. It isn't far at all.
67. Par ici.	This way.
68. Par là.	That way.
69. Va tout droit. **(Allez tout droit.)**	Go straight ahead.
70. Tourne à droite. **(Tournez à droite.)**	Turn right.
71. Tourne à gauche. **(Tournez à gauche.)**	Turn left.
72. Au feu	At the light
73. Continue. **(Continuez.)**	Keep going. Continue.
74. Prends la première rue... **(Prenez la premiere rue...)**	Take the first street...
75. Arrête! **(Arrêtez!)**	Stop!
76. Le (La) voilà!	There it is!

Here's a conversation illustrating many of these expressions:

Mark Davis, an exchange student from the United States, is trying to find a bank in Épône, a small town near Paris. He approaches an elderly gentleman, M. Martin, and asks for directions:

MARK: Pardonnez-moi, Monsieur. Où est la banque, s'il vous plaît?

M. MARTIN: Ce n'est pas loin d'ici. Tournez à gauche au feu...puis prenez la deuxième rue à droite...et la voilà à côté du supermarché. C'est tout près.

MARK: Tournez à gauche au feu...puis prenez la deuxième rue à droite?

M. MARTIN: Oui, c'est ça!

MARK: Merci beaucoup, Monsieur.

M. MARTIN: De rien, Monsieur.

Notice that Mark repeated the directions. This is an important strategy, which gives him a chance to verify that he has understood them. If there is something he has misunderstood, M. Martin will undoubtedly correct the mistake.

If your destination is not very far away, you occasionally will hear the following expression:

77. Suis-moi.   Follow me.
(Suivez-moi.)

Sometimes people are so friendly that they will personally escort you to your destination. On the other hand, if your destination is too far to walk to, you will often hear:

78. Il vaudrait mieux   You're better off taking a
prendre un taxi (le   taxi (the subway).
métro).

If you do take a cab, say the following when tipping the driver:

79. Voilà...pour vous.   Here's a little something
                               for you.

By the way, if you're in France, be sure to buy copies of the Michelin Guide. It will provide you with detailed information on the region you are visiting. Another good idea is to stop at the *Syndicat d'Initiative* (the tourist information center) for brochures and friendly advice about the area. Look for the "T" sign outside the office.

II. Application

A. If you had to ask for directions, what would you do in each of the following situations? (Be certain to follow the advice of the person giving directions.)

1. SITUATION   You are in Paris at the Palais du Luxembourg on the Left Bank. You're trying to get to the Gare St-Lazare (a train station on the Right Bank), so you ask the first person you see:

YOU SAY: Pardonnez-moi, Madame. Est-ce que la Gare St-Lazare est près d'ici?

YOU HEAR: Mais non. La Gare St-Lazare est loin d'ici sur la rive droite. Il vaudrait mieux prendre le métro. La station est près d'ici...La voilà...et il faut consulter le plan à l'entrée du métro.

> According to the directions you have been given, it would be best to
> > a. Walk to the train station.
> > b. Take the subway to the train station.
> > c. Take a taxi.

2. SITUATION You are driving to a meeting at the Château Frontenac, a prestigious hotel in the city of Quebec. You roll down your window and ask someone in the next car where it's located:

YOU SAY: Pardonnez-moi. Où se trouve le Château Frontenac, s'il vous plaît?

YOU HEAR: Tournez à droite au feu...et le voilà à gauche. C'est tout près.

> According to the directions you have been given, it would be best to
> > a. Turn right at the light and then start looking for a place to park your car.
> > b. Turn right at the light and then turn left.
> > c. Park your car and take a bus.

3. SITUATION You are in Fort-de-France, the capital of the beautiful island of Martinique in the Caribbean. You need some tourist information, so you ask for directions to the tourist office:

YOU SAY: Excusez-moi, Mademoiselle. Pouvez-vous me dire comment aller au Syndicat d'Initiative, s'il vous plaît?

YOU HEAR: Oh là là! Au Syndicat d'Initiative?...Voyons...Ah oui! Allez tout droit jusqu'au deuxième...Non, non,...au troisième feu...et puis tournez à gauche...Non, non,...à droite. Continuez tout droit...ou tournez à droite ...peut-être. J'en suis désolée Monsieur, mais je ne suis pas sûre.

> According to the information you have been given, it would be best to
> > a. Try to follow the directions as given.
> > b. Take the bus.
> > c. Try asking someone else for directions before doing anything else.

B. Look at the map below. Do the directions on the left take you to the stadium, the café, or the mall? Start from *X*.

Tournez à gauche au feu et allez tout droit...et puis prenez la troisième rue à gauche...et le voilà à droite.

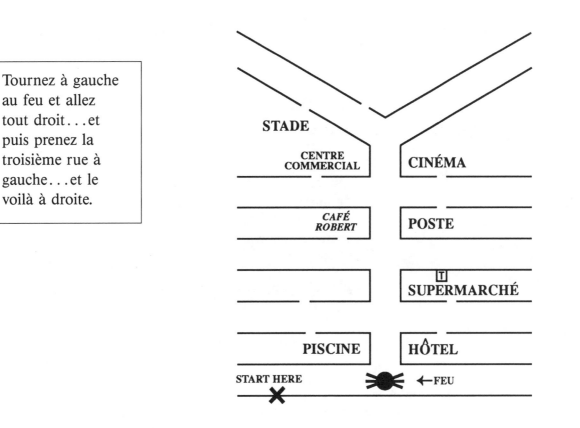

III. Amusez-vous!

Aveugle Perdu

Here is a great classroom game you can play to practice some of the expressions you have learned in this lesson. To play it you need a blindfold and your teacher's permission to rearrange the room. The game is played in teams of three, with one team competing at a time. The object of the game is to direct a blindfolded teammate—using only French expressions—through a maze of obstacles. The blindfolded person should touch as few obstacles as possible. A point is scored *against* your team for each of the following violations: the blindfolded teammate touches an obstacle with any part of his or her body, or an attempt is made to communicate with the blindfolded person in English or by touch. The team with the lowest score wins. Remember, all communication must be in French.

Suggested expressions for Aveugle Perdu are

Tournez à gauche.	**Un peu.**
Tournez à droite.	**Continuez.**
Allez tout droit.	**Arrêtez!**

IV. Take These with You	**61. Je me suis perdu (perdue).**	I'm lost.
	62. Peux-tu me dire comment aller à l'hôpital? (Pouvez-vous me dire comment aller à l'hôpital?)	Can you tell me how to get to the hospital?
	63. Est-ce que l'hôpital est près d'ici?	Is the hospital nearby?
	64. Où se trouve l'hôpital?	Where is the hospital?
	65. C'est loin d'ici.	It's far away.
	66. C'est tout près.	It's nearby. It isn't far at all.
	67. Par ici.	This way.
	68. Par là.	That way.
	69. Va tout droit. (Allez tout droit.)	Go straight ahead.
	70. Tourne à droite. (Tournez à droite.)	Turn right.
	71. Tourne à gauche. (Tournez à gauche.)	Turn left.
	72. Au feu	At the light

73. **Continue.** (**Continuez.**)	Keep going. Continue.
74. **Prends la première rue...** (**Prenez la première rue...**)	Take the first street...
75. **Arrête!** (**Arrêtez!**)	Stop!
76. **Le (La) voilà!**	There it is!
77. **Suis-moi.** (**Suivez-moi.**)	Follow me.
78. **Il vaudrait mieux prendre un taxi (le métro).**	You're better off taking a taxi (the subway).
79. **Voilà...pour vous.**	Here's a little something for you.

LESSON NINE   Talking on the Telephone

There's no question that the art of using a telephone is critical to socializing and to successfully conducting business in today's world. Telephone conversations can be trickier than ordinary conversations because you can't see the person you're talking to. It's much more difficult to understand when you don't see the hand gestures and facial expressions people use when talking. It would be well worth your while to practice the expressions presented in this lesson until they become automatic. This will enable you to concentrate more on the message itself when you're talking on the phone in French. Finally, don't forget to review what you should do when you're confused or don't understand, as covered in Lesson 4.

I. What to Say Imagine that you are in France visiting your cousins Louis and Andrée (ages 16 and 6 respectively). A little after eight o'clock in the evening the phone rings, and you answer it.

(Drin, drin)

You pick up the receiver and say:

80. Allô.   Hello.

To find out who is calling, you ask:

81. Qui est à l'appareil?   Who is it?

The person calling first says, **Allô** and then identifies himself or herself by saying:

82. Ici Pierre.   This is Pierre.

He then uses *Blanches #19* to ask to speak to Louis:

Je voudrais parler à Louis.

Next he asks:

83. Est-ce qu'il (elle) est là?   Is he (she) in?

You've been up in your room reading a book and you really don't know if your cousin is at home or not, so you decide to ask Andrée. First you tell Pierre:

84. Ne quitte pas.   Hang on.
(Ne quittez pas.)

Andrée tells you that Louis went for a bike ride, but she doesn't know where. So you inform Pierre:

85. Il (Elle) n'est pas là.   He's (She's) not in.

Then you ask:

86. Veux-tu laisser un message? (**Voulez-vous laisser un message?**)	Do you want to leave a message?

Pierre doesn't have a message to leave. He merely wants to talk to Louis about the party he's giving Saturday night, so he says:

87. Je vais rappeler plus tard.	I'll call back later.

Next, Pierre asks when you think Louis will return:

88. Quand sera-t-il (elle) de retour?	When will he (she) be back?

Unfortunately, Andrée has turned up the volume on the TV, making it impossible to hear Pierre's question, so you say:

89. Pardon, je ne peux pas t'entendre (vous entendre).	I'm sorry, I can't hear you.

And then:

90. Un peu plus fort, s'il vous plaît.	A little louder, please.

Pierre repeats his question and you still can't hear, so you shout to Andrée:

91. La télé, moins fort!	Turn down the TV!

After apologizing to Pierre with *Bleues #10,*

J'en suis désolée, you say:

92. Tu disais...? (**Vous disiez...?**)	You were saying...?

Pierre repeats his question, and you explain that you don't know when Louis will be back. Then he says:

93. Ce n'est pas urgent.   It's not important.

Realizing that you must be Louis's cousin who is visiting from the United States, Pierre asks you how you are enjoying your stay in France. Then he invites you to his party. You're interested in going, and you want to catch all the details:

94. Va...je t'écoute.   Go on...I'm listening.
(Allez...je vous
écoute.)

You tell Pierre that you'll think it over and that you'll let him know tomorrow whether you can go. Your cousin Andrée is calling you, so you say:

95. Il faut que je   I have to hang up.
raccroche.

Pierre would like to get your answer as soon as possible, so he says:

96. Rappelle-moi tout de   Call me back right away.
suite.
(Rappelez-moi tout de
suite.)

Finally, you tell Pierre that you'll tell Louis that he called, and then you say good-bye.

II. Application

A. Select the most appropriate expression for each of the following situations:

1. Your friend Latoya was absent from school today, so you call her to find out how she's feeling. Unfortunately, she has laryngitis, and it's too much of an effort for her to talk. You tell her:

    a. Je vais rappeler plus tard.

    b. Elle n'est pas là.

    c. Voulez-vous laisser un message?

2. Someone calls and wants to speak to your brother. You're not sure which of his friends is calling, so you ask:

    a. Quand sera-t-il de retour?

    b. Tu disais. . .?

    c. Qui est à l'appareil?

3. Mme Mathiot, your dad's boss, would like to speak to him about a business matter. Your dad is working in the yard, so you say:

    a. La télé, moins fort!

    b. Ne quittez pas, Madame, s'il vous plaît.

    c. Ce n'est pas urgent.

4. You're planning a surprise birthday party for your mom this Saturday. Your Aunt Sylvie calls to get the details, but you

have to hang up because you can hear your mom about to enter the room. Before hanging up you whisper:

    a. Va...je t'écoute.

    b. Il faut que je raccroche. Maman arrive. Je vais rappeler plus tard.

    c. Ne quitte pas, Tante Sylvie. Maman arrive.

5. There was an explosion in the school chemistry lab and one of the students, Jean-Luc Cartier, was seriously injured. You're the school principal, so you call Jean-Luc's home to notify his parents of the accident. No one is home, so you leave the following message on their answering machine:

    a. Ici M. Duvalier, le directeur de l'école...Jean-Luc ne peut pas déjeuner aujourd'hui. Il a oublié son argent. Rappelez-moi au 555-4387 le plus tôt possible. C'est urgent.

    b. Ici M. Duvalier, le directeur de l'école...Rappelez-moi au 555-4387 le plus tôt possible. Jean-Luc n'est pas là aujourd'hui.

    c. Ici M. Duvalier, le directeur de l'école...Il y a eu un accident aujourd'hui et Jean-Luc est à l'hôpital. Rappelez-moi au 555-4387 le plus tôt possible. C'est urgent.

B. After reading the following telephone conversation, complete the message form below as accurately as possible. Use today's date and current time when filling out the form:

SECRÉTAIRE: Allô.

JACQUES GUILLEMARD: Allô. Je voudrais parler à M. Dufour, s'il vous plaît.

SECRÉTAIRE: Qui est à l'appareil?

JACQUES GUILLEMARD: Ici Jacques Guillemard de la Société de Martin et Lebrun de New York.

SECRÉTAIRE: J'en suis désolée, mais M. Dufour n'est pas là maintenant. Voulez-vous laisser un message?

JACQUES GUILLEMARD: Oui. Je vous en prie. Dites à M. Dufour que j'arrive à Paris demain et je voudrais qu'il me rencontre à l'aéroport.

SECRÉTAIRE: À quelle heure, Monsieur?

JACQUES GUILLEMARD: J'arrive demain matin à l'aéroport Charles de Gaulle à dix heures et quart...vol n°327...Air France.

SECRÉTAIRE: D'accord, Monsieur.

JACQUES GUILLEMARD: S'il ne peut pas me rencontrer, il peut me rappeler à (212) 555-9483, l'interne 25. Est-ce que vous voudriez que je répète le numéro?

SECRÉTAIRE: Non, ce n'est pas nécessaire. Je lui donnerai le message.

JACQUES GUILLEMARD: Merci beaucoup, Madame.

SECRÉTAIRE: Il n'y a pas de quoi, Monsieur. Au revoir.

JACQUES GUILLEMARD: Au revoir.

Pendant votre absence

à_____

date_____ heure_____

M. / Mme / Mlle_____

téléphone_____

    ☐ veuillez rappeler   ☐ rappellera

Message_____

_____

_____

_____

_____

téléphoniste_____

III. Amusez-vous!   Here's the message you hear on your friend David's answering machine:

Allô. Ici David. Je suis occupé maintenant, mais vous pouvez laisser un message et je vous rappellerai le plus tôt possible. Veuillez donner votre nom et votre numéro de téléphone. Attendez le ton. Merci.

You have only twenty seconds to leave your name, telephone number, and message. In this activity you are expected to leave the message outlined below within the twenty-second time period. Include your own name and telephone number in the blanks below.

YOU SAY: Allô. Ici _____ . Est-ce que tu voudrais aller avec moi au cinéma samedi soir? Si tu peux aller, donne-moi un coup de téléphone tout de suite. Mon numéro de téléphone est _____ . Merci. Au revoir.

Scoring: If you can read the entire message within twenty seconds or less, you will receive a perfect score of twenty points. One point for each second over the twenty-second maximum will be deducted from your score.

Examples: 17 seconds = 20 points; 18 seconds = 20 points; 20 seconds = 20 points; 25 seconds = 15 points; 28 seconds = 12 points.

Work in teams. Compare your scores.

IV. Take These with You

80.	**Allô.**	Hello.
81.	**Qui est à l'appareil?**	Who is it?
82.	**Ici Pierre.**	This is Pierre.
83.	**Est-ce qu'il (elle) est là?**	Is he (she) in?
84.	**Ne quitte pas.** **(Ne quittez pas.)**	Hang on.
85.	**Il (Elle) n'est pas là.**	He (She)'s not in.
86.	**Veux-tu laisser un message?** **(Voulez-vous laisser un message?)**	Do you want to leave a message?
87.	**Je vais rappeler plus tard.**	I'll call back later.

88. Quand sera-t-il (elle) de retour?	When will he (she) be back?
89. Pardon, je ne peux pas t'entendre (vous entendre).	I'm sorry, I can't hear you.
90. Un peu plus fort, s'il vous plaît.	A little louder, please.
91. La télé, moins fort!	Turn down the TV!
92. Tu disais...? (Vous disiez...?)	You were saying...?
93. Ce n'est pas urgent.	It's not important.
94. Va...je t'écoute. (Allez, je vous écoute.)	Go on...I'm listening.
95. Il faut que je raccroche.	I have to hang up.
96. Rappelle-moi tout de suite. (Rappelez-moi tout de suite.)	Call me back right away.

LOCUTIONS ROUGES:
Getting Along with Others

LESSON TEN **Making Friends**

The final set of expressions, the *Locutions Rouges,* are probably the most interesting in this book because they are generally designed to help you make friends or get along better with the friends you already have. Lesson 10 deals with the art of meeting people and with being polite. It also covers different ways of saying good-bye.

I. What to Say ***Saying Hello and Meeting People***

You have undoubtedly learned to greet others by saying **Bonjour.** If you are going out in the evening, or just meeting people after sunset, you can also greet them with:

1. Bonsoir   Good evening.

You also know how to ask how things are going with **Comment allez-vous?** or perhaps **Ça va?** Here are a few other popular expressions that can be used only among friends:

2. Salut!   Hi!

3. Ça marche?   How's it going?
(**Ça marche?** is especially
popular in Canada.)

4. Quoi de neuf?   What's new?

Perhaps you would like to introduce someone to a friend. This can easily be accomplished by saying:

5. Je te présente mon ami Jean.	I'd like you to meet my friend John.
(Je vous présente mon amie Jeanne.)	I'd like you to meet my friend Jeanne.

In order to express how happy you are to meet the person to whom you are being introduced, you can say:

6. Très heureux (heureuse) de faire votre connaissance.	I'm very happy to meet you.

Of course, it's easier just to say:

7. Enchanté(e).	Pleased to meet you.

If you're having a **boum** (*party*), you might welcome a guest by saying:

8. Bienvenu(e)	Welcome

If you would like to socialize at a party, you might try asking someone to dance:

9. Tu danses?	Do you want to dance?

One way to accept an invitation to do so is

10. Pourquoi pas?	Why not?

Being Polite

You've already been using several of the most important expressions for being polite when learning the *Locutions Blanches #1–6*.

Blanches #1	**Je t'en prie.**	
	(Je vous en prie.)	
		Please.
Blanches #2	**S'il vous plaît.**	

Blanches #3	**Excuse-moi.** **(Excusez-moi.)**	Excuse me.
Blanches #4	**Je m'excuse.**	
Blanches #5	**Pardon.**	
Blanches #6	**Pardonne-moi.** **(Pardonnez-moi.)**	Pardon me.

To these we should add a few others:

11. Merci beaucoup.   Thank you very much.

12. Merci mille fois.   Thanks a million.
                             (literally: *a thousand*)

13. Il n'y a pas de quoi.

14. Pas de quoi.   You're welcome.

15. De rien.

Blanches #1, **Je t'en prie./Je vous en prie** can also mean *You're welcome.*

When asking permission in French, you should use

16. Puis-je?   May I?
                     Can I?

Here are some examples:

Puis-je aller au cinéma ce soir?
Puis-je regarder la télé maintenant; j'ai déjà fini mes devoirs.
Puis-je vous aider, Mademoiselle?

(Note that in French, **Puis-je?** means both *May I* and *Can I.* This means you don't have to worry about making a grammar mistake by saying *Can I?* when you really mean *May I?,* as in English.)

Saying Good-Bye

There are a number of ways to say good-bye. Certainly you already know **Au revoir.** Here are some other common expressions:

17. À bientôt.	See you soon.
18. À demain.	See you tomorrow.
19. À tout à l'heure.	See you later.

And here are some special expressions:

20. Bon voyage!	Have a nice trip!
21. Bonne nuit.	Good night.

When saying good night, don't forget to add:

22. Fais de beaux rêves! **(Faites de beaux rêves!)**	Sweet dreams!

II. Application   A. Select the most appropriate expression for each of the following situations:

1. You're walking with a friend to your next class. She drops all her books, and you help her pick them up. She thanks you for helping her, so you say:
   a. Bonne nuit.
   b. Bon voyage!
   c. Pas de quoi.

2. Your friend Louis introduces you to his cousin Catherine who is visiting from Trois-Rivières, Québec. Showing how happy you are to meet her, you say:

    a. De rien.

    b. Enchanté(e).

    c. Merci mille fois.

3. You notice a woman having trouble loading up her car with groceries in the supermarket parking lot. Her bags burst, so you offer to help her out by asking:

    a. Tu danses?

    b. Puis-je vous aider, Madame?

    c. Quoi de neuf, Madame?

4. You're babysitting for your four-year-old nephew, Billy. It's Billy's bedtime, and you tell him he should go to bed. Billy gives you a hug and says good night. You also say good night and add:

    a. Fais de beaux rêves, Billy!

    b. Très heureux de faire votre connaissance, Billy.

    c. Il n'y a pas de quoi, Billy.

5. An hour past his bedtime, Billy comes downstairs and asks for his fifth drink of water. Losing patience with your nephew, you urge him to get back to bed by saying:

    a. J'ai soif, Tonton Robert!

    b. Bonne nuit, Billy. À demain!

    c. Enchanté, Billy!

B. Complete the following responses based on the expressions discussed in this lesson. Choose your answers from the words in the box given:

1. Merci mille fois, Gustave.

    —De _____ .

2. Christine, je te présente mon ami Pierre.

—Très _____ de _____

votre _____ .

3. Bonne nuit, Maman.

— _____ de beaux _____ .

4. Oh là là! Ma classe commence et je suis en retard!

—À _____ à l' _____ , Marie.

5. Bonsoir, André! Ça marche?

— _____ , Denise! Oui, ça _____ .

Et toi?

6. Robert et moi, nous allons faire un voyage en France. Nous
partons demain.

—Bon _____ !

rêves	marche	connaissance
salut	rien	heureuse
fais	tout	heure
faire	voyage	

III. Amusez-vous!   Which of the words in the box below best completes the following joke? Write your answer in the space provided:

Un morceau de sucre adore une petite cuiller:

<<Je voudrais un rendez-vous avec toi>>, demande le sucre,

<<mais je ne sais pas où>>.

La cuiller répond cruellement:

<<Je ne sais pas, peut-être dans un _____ >>.

restaurant   bistro   café

IV. Take These with You

1. **Salut!**	Hi!
2. **Bonsoir.**	Good evening.
3. **Ça marche?**	How's it going?
4. **Quoi de neuf?**	What's new?
5. **Je te présente mon ami Jean.** (**Je vous présente mon amie Jeanne.**)	I'd like you to meet my friend Jean. (I'd like you to meet my friend Jeanne.)
6. **Très heureux (heureuse) de faire votre connaissance.**	I'm very happy to meet you.
7. **Enchanté(e).**	Pleased to meet you.
8. **Bienvenu(e)**	Welcome
9. **Tu danses?**	Do you want to dance?
10. **Pourquoi pas?**	Why not?

11. **Merci beaucoup.**	Thank you very much.
12. **Merci mille fois.**	Thanks a million. (literally: *a thousand*)
13. **Il n'y a pas de quoi.**	
14. **Pas de quoi.**	You're welcome.
15. **De rien.**	
16. **Puis-je?**	May I? Can I?
17. **À bientôt.**	See you soon.
18. **À demain.**	See you tomorrow.
19. **À tout à l'heure.**	See you later.
20. **Bon voyage!**	Have a nice trip!
21. **Bonne nuit.**	Good night.
22. **Fais de beaux rêves!** (**Faites de beaux rêves!**)	Sweet dreams!

LESSON ELEVEN   ## Saying Yes, No, and Maybe

How do you say no to a friend who wants you to do something you don't want to do? How should you say yes to someone who offers to do you a big favor? Sometimes "Yes" and "No" just aren't adequate for the subtleties of social interaction.

Lesson 11 will spice up your French by providing you with a few more options to choose from when you have to say <<Oui>> or <<Non>>.

I. What to Say

Saying Yes

Whenever you hear a question beginning with the expression **Est-ce que...**, the speaker is usually expecting an answer of either **Oui** or **Non.** What answer would you give if someone asked you this question?:

> **Est-ce que** vous voudriez faire un voyage en France cet été, si vous aviez l'argent?

Since you are a student of French, you probably would say **Oui.** A simple yes answer, however, would not give any indication of enthusiasm.

Here are a few other ways of saying yes. Notice how each conveys a different attitude, ranging from apathy to enthusiasm.

23. D'accord.	OK.
	I agree.
24. Bien entendu.	Of course.
25. Volontiers!	Gladly!
26. Il n'y a pas d'erreur.	There's no doubt about it.

And don't forget:

Bleues #21	**Et comment!**	You bet!
		And how!

Which would *you* use to answer yes to the above question?

_____

When a friend asks you to do him or her a favor, you can use any of the above expressions or say:

27. Compte sur moi.	You can count on me.
(Comptez sur moi.)	

For example:

VOTRE AMI: Est-ce que tu peux aller au concert avec Marie samedi soir? Voici les billets. Je ne peux pas y aller.

VOUS: **Volontiers! Compte sur moi.**

Here's how you can agree with someone who likes something you like:

28. Moi aussi.	Me too. So do I.

Example:

VOTRE AMIE: Moi, j'adore les escargots.

VOUS: **Moi aussi.**

Here's how you can agree with someone who shares a dislike for something:

29. Ni moi non plus.	Neither do I.

Example:

VOTRE AMI: Moi, je n'aime pas les pantalons à patte d'éléphant *(bell-bottoms)*.

VOUS: **Ni moi non plus!**

Remember to avoid using the word **oui** to contradict negative questions. Imagine, for example, that after having worked for weeks on a social-studies project, your father is under the impression that you haven't even begun:

VOTRE PÈRE: Comment? Tu n'as pas encore commencé ton projet!

In this case, you should avoid answering **Oui, Papa.** If you do, you are agreeing with your dad and saying that you have *not* yet started to work on the project. Expression #30 is the shortest one in *Au courant* but it's an important one.

30. Si.	Yes (when contradicting negative questions).

A good way of answering your dad would be to say:

Si, Papa. Le projet est presque fini!

Saying No

Here are a handful of expressions you can use to say no:

31. Ce n'est pas la peine!	It isn't worth the trouble.
32. Ce n'est pas ton affaire!	It's none of your business!
33. Je ne suis pas né(e) d'hier!	I wasn't born yesterday!
34. Jamais de la vie!	Out of the question!
35. Tu peux toujours courir! (**Vous pouvez toujours courir!**)	You can take a flying leap!

Which of the above expressions would you use to warn a friend not to go to a sale at the mall? You went last night and they were already all sold out.

_____

Which expression do you think would be best for telling someone you don't want to do something foolish, such as taking a shortcut across a lake of thin ice?

_____

They say that there are two sides to every story. The following expression can come in handy when you want to discuss something from a second point of view:

36. Au contraire	On the contrary

For example:

LAURENT: Je n'aime pas l'hiver. Il n'y a rien à faire.

VOUS: **Au contraire,** Laurent, en hiver on peut faire du patinage ou faire du ski, et on peut jouer au hockey aussi.

Saying Maybe

We have already discussed a few good expressions to be used when further discussion is needed to make up your mind:

Bleues #26	**Peut-être.**	Maybe. Perhaps.
Bleues #27	**Ça dépend.**	That depends.
Bleues #28	**Ça dépend de toi.** (**Ça dépend de vous.**)	That depends on you.

Here's an expression you can use to play "devil's advocate":

37. Par contre   On the other hand

For example:

ANNICK: On peut jouer au tennis aujourd'hui. Qu'en penses-tu?

VOUS: Quelle bonne idée, Annick! **Par contre,** on peut aller au cinéma. J'ai entendu dire qu'il va pleuvoir cet après-midi.

Notice how **Au contraire** conveys a definite opposition to a particular point of view. **Par contre,** on the other hand, leaves plenty of room for discussion. Would you use **Au contraire** or **Par contre** in the following situation? Write your answer in the blank below:

GILLES: Le drapeau français est bleu, blanc et vert, n'est-ce pas?

VOUS: _____ , Gilles. Le drapeau français est bleu, blanc et rouge.

Here are three great expressions to be used when trying to be cautious. To make these expressions negative, change the **oui** to **non**:

38. Je pense que oui.   I think so.
    Je pense que non.   I don't think so.

39. Je crois que oui.   I believe so.
    Je crois que non.   I don't believe so.

40. J'espère que oui.   I hope so.
    J'espère que non.   I hope not.

Using *Rouges #38–#40* or their negative counterparts, which would you choose to react to the following?

VOTRE MÈRE: Vite! Venez, tout le monde! Vite! On a dit à la télé que quelqu'un de notre village a gagné le gros lot à la Loterie Nationale...Peut-être c'est nous! Le ticket est dans mon sac à main...Oh là là, je ne peux pas le trouver...Où est le ticket? Peut-être je l'ai perdu!

VOUS: _____

II. Application   A. Select the most appropriate expression for each of the following situations:

1. Your next door neighbor has an emergency, and she needs someone to watch her six-year-old daughter for a few hours. There's no question that you would like to help out, so you agree by saying:

   a. Ça dépend.

   b. Jamais de la vie!

   c. Comptez sur moi.

2. A classmate, Mathieu, would like you to do him a big favor. He'd like you to lend him your car so that he can take Natalie to the party you're throwing this Friday night. He knows very well that you are interested in Natalie yourself. In fact, you were planning to invite Natalie to the party tonight. You tell Mathieu that you don't want to lend him your car by saying:

   a. Volontiers!

   b. Je crois que oui.

   c. Tu peux toujours courir!

3. Mathieu thinks he can borrow someone else's car, but he has forgotten Natalie's phone number. He asks you if you would give him her number. You say:

   a. Ce n'est pas ton affaire!

   b. D'accord. Je peux sortir avec Natalie une autre fois.

   c. Il n'y a pas d'erreur.

4. Natalie and her friend Chantal are discussing their plans for this Friday night. Chantal says she wishes she could go to the big party but she can't. Natalie has to stay home too because relatives from out of town are coming to visit. Natalie says:

   a. Tu ne peux pas y aller? Je ne suis pas née d'hier... Tu vas à la boum avec Mathieu, n'est-ce pas?

   b. Tu ne peux pas y aller? Ni moi non plus. Peut-être une autre fois.

   c. Est-ce que je vais à la boum? Ce n'est pas ton affaire!

5. After you have bought a new shirt at the Printemps department store in Paris, an employee who thinks you may be leaving the store without paying for the shirt approaches and asks: <<Vous n'avez pas de reçu pour cette chemise, n'est-ce pas?>> You reach into the bag and produce the receipt, saying:

    a. Si, Monsieur. Le voici.
    b. Oui, Monsieur.
    c. J'espère que oui.

B. Show how you personally would react to each of the questions or statements below, without using *oui* or *non*. Use any of the expressions discussed in this lesson, and try not to repeat any of your answers:

1. De quelle couleur sont les sous-vêtements que vous portez aujourd'hui?

_____

2. Est-ce qu'on parle français à Ottawa, la capitale du Canada?

_____

3. Washington, DC est la capitale des États-Unis.

_____

4. Est-ce que vous ne comprenez pas la différence entre <<oui>> et <<si>>?

_____

5. Moi, je voudrais faire un voyage en Martinique cet été. Et vous?

_____

6. Les garçons sont plus sportifs que les filles.

_____

7. Oh là là! J'ai entendu qu'il y a eu un accident nucléaire près de Chicago. Est-ce vrai?

_____

8. Zut! J'ai oublié d'acheter un journal, mais il faut retourner à l'autre côté du centre commercial pour l'acheter.

_____

9. Pouvez-vous me dire comment aller à l'hôpital?

_____

10. Savez-vous qui est le président de la France?

_____

III. Amusez-vous!   *Trivia Question*

Do you know the name of the only American to win the *Tour de France,* the world's most important bicycle race? He won it in 1986, 1989 and 1990.

Using the clues at the bottom of the page, complete the following puzzle to find the answer:

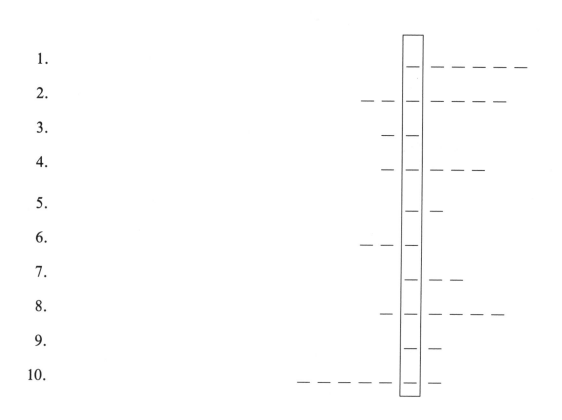

1. English equivalent of **Volontiers.**

2. **Peut-être** means "Maybe" or "_____ ."

3. Je ne suis pas _____ d'hier.

4. **D'accord** means "OK" or "I _____ ."

5. Ce n'est pas _____ peine!

6. Jamais de la _____ !

7. _____ aussi.

8. Par _____ .

9. _____ moi non plus.

10. Bien _____ .

IV. Take These with You

23. **D'accord.**	OK. I agree.
24. **Bien entendu.**	Of course.
25. **Volontiers!**	Gladly!
26. **Il n'y a pas d'erreur.**	There's no doubt about it.
27. **Compte sur moi.** **(Comptez sur moi.)**	You can count on me.
28. **Moi aussi.**	Me too. So do I.
29. **Ni moi non plus.**	Neither do I.
30. **Si.**	Yes (when contradicting a negative question).
31. **Ce n'est pas la peine!**	It isn't worth the trouble.
32. **Ce n'est pas ton affaire!**	It's none of your business!
33. **Je ne suis pas né(e) d'hier!**	I wasn't born yesterday!
34. **Jamais de la vie!**	Out of the question!
35. **Tu peux toujours courir!** **(Vous pouvez toujours courir!)**	You can take a flying leap!
36. **Au contraire**	On the contrary
37. **Par contre**	On the other hand
38. **Je pense que oui.** **Je pense que non.**	I think so. I don't think so.
39. **Je crois que oui.** **Je crois que non.**	I believe so. I don't believe so.
40. **J'espère que oui.** **J'espère que non.**	I hope so. I hope not.

LESSON TWELVE   Making Plans

People who speak foreign languages usually are very active people because they generally have many opportunities to socialize and to enjoy new experiences. The expressions you learn in this lesson will help you make plans with your friends. You will also learn how to invite someone out and what to say when someone invites you out.

I. What to Say

What to Do?

When you find yourself repeating the following expression, you know it's time to find a friend and start planning something to take the boredom out of your life:

41. Il n'y a rien à faire.	There's nothing to do.

Here's how you say what you would like to do:

42. J'ai envie de...	I feel like...
43. J'ai l'intention de... Or perhaps:	I plan to...
44. J'aimerais mieux...	I'd rather...

How would you say that you feel like going to the beach this afternoon?

_____

How would you say that you are planning to go horseback riding Tuesday morning?

_____

In discussing your plans, you might like to reminisce about some interesting (or awful) experiences you have had in the past:

45. La dernière fois	The last time
46. Au passé	In the past

Au passé, nous nagions dans ce lac tous les weekends.

If an outing doesn't go well, you'll have to do something else the next time:

47. La prochaine fois   The next time

48. À l'avenir   In the future

La prochaine fois, on va faire autre chose. Ce lac est trop contaminé!

Invitations

French teenagers are not very "date-conscious." They like to go out, usually in groups, just to have a good time. When you go to France, you'll probably use this set of expressions a great deal.
Here's how to ask someone to go out with you:

49. Est-ce que tu es libre? (Est-ce que vous êtes libre?)   Are you doing anything?

50. Est-ce que tu voudrais aller avec moi au cinéma? (Est-ce que vous voudriez aller avec moi au cinéma?)   Would you like to go with me to the movies?

How would you ask someone if she's doing anything after school?

How would you ask a friend if he would like to go with you to a football game this Saturday afternoon?

_____

_____

You already know a variety of ways to accept an invitation:

Bleues #21	**Et comment!**	You bet! And how!
Bleues #22	**Avec plaisir!**	With pleasure!
Rouges #10	**Pourquoi pas?**	Why not?
Rouges #23	**D'accord.**	OK. I agree.
Rouges #24	**Bien entendu.**	Of course.
Rouges #25	**Volontiers!**	Gladly!

It's usually very easy to accept an invitation. Turning someone down, on the other hand, can often be much more difficult. To decline an invitation, you can use either of the following:

51. Malheureusement, je ne peux pas.	Unfortunately, I can't.
52. Peut-être une autre fois.	Perhaps some other time.

It's normally polite to offer a reason or an excuse. Here are a few of the most common:

53. Je n'ai pas le temps.	I don't have the time.
54. Je n'ai pas l'argent.	I don't have the money.
55. Je suis occupé(e).	I'm busy.

If you're worried about being late, you can hurry your friends along by saying:

56. On y va.

Let's get going.

57. Allons-y.

When it's getting late and you have to leave, you can say:

58. Il faut que j'aille.

I have to get going.

59. Il faut que je parte.

Emergencies

When you're having fun with your friends, let's hope that nothing unfortunate ever happens to spoil your fun. Just in case something does, though, these emergency expressions might come in handy:

60. Au voleur!   Stop, thief!

61. Au feu!   Fire!

And finally, the most important:

62. Au secours!   Help!

II. Application

A. Select the most appropriate expression for each of the following situations:

1. Your dad is picking you up at 4:00 P.M. in front of the school. It's already 3:50 P.M. and you're still shooting baskets with your friends in the gym. You have to take a shower yet, so you tell your friends:

   a. Je n'ai pas l'argent.

   b. Il faut que je parte.

   c. Au voleur!

2. Your mother is celebrating her fortieth birthday this Saturday, and you and your sister want to throw her a big party. Your friend Michel calls and asks you if you would like to go with him to an amusement park this Saturday. Since you can't go with him you say:

   a. Avec plaisir.

   b. Peut-être une autre fois, Michel. Je suis occupé samedi après-midi.

   c. Je ne peux pas, Michel. Je n'ai pas l'argent.

3. You and your cousin are shopping at the Galeries Lafayette in Paris. While taking the escalator to the second floor, your cousin's shoelace gets caught, and in an effort to get someone to quickly shut the escalator down, she yells:

   a. Au feu! L'escalier roulant a pris feu!

   b. Au voleur! Cet homme-là a volé mon paquet!

   c. Au secours! Je me suis accrochée (*caught*)! Coupez l'électricité! Vite!

4. You and your friends are discussing what you would like to do this weekend. Gabriel would like to go to the video arcade Saturday afternoon. You don't think it's such a good idea, so you say:

    a. Je n'ai rien à faire.

    b. À mon avis, ce n'est pas une bonne idée. La dernière fois il y avait trop de monde.

    c. Pourquoi pas? Allons-y!

5. You'd like to invite Valérie to go with you to the party at Roger's house this Friday night, so you call her and ask:

    a. Valérie, est-ce que tu voudrais aller avec moi à la boum chez Roger vendredi soir?

    b. Valérie, est-ce que tu es libre mardi matin? Il y a une boum chez Roger.

    c. Valérie, est-ce que tu voudrais aller à la boum chez Roger vendredi soir? Malheureusement, je ne peux pas y aller.

B. Complete the following based on the expressions discussed in this lesson.

1. Qu'est-ce que tu voudrais faire ce weekend, Micheline?

    —J'ai _____ de faire du ski, Pierre.

2. Est-ce que tu voudrais aller _____ moi au centre commercial cet après-midi, Colette?

    —Malheureusement, je ne _____ pas parce qu'il faut que j'étudie cet après-midi.

3. Fiston, pourquoi est-ce que tu as l'air triste?

    —Il n'y a _____ à _____ , Maman.

4. Est-ce que vous _____ aller faire du ski dimanche après-midi?

    —Jamais de la vie! J'aimerais _____ faire du patinage parce que le ski est trop dangereux.

5. Robert, est-ce que tu voudrais aller au concert avec moi la semaine prochaine?

—J'en suis désolé, Hélène, mais je n'ai pas l' _____ .

Peut-être, une _____ fois.

III. Amusez-vous!   Ten popular excuses are listed below. Find out what they are by solving the following puzzle:

Excuses! Excuses! Excuses!

ACROSS

3. C'est trop _____ .

4. Je suis trop _____ .

5. Je suis _____ .

7. Je n'ai pas le _____ .

9. J'ai une _____ .

10. Je ne _____ pas.

DOWN

2. Je suis _____ .

2. Je n'ai pas l' _____ .

6. Je ne _____ pas.

8. Je ne suis pas _____ .

IV. Take These with You

41.	Il n'y a rien à faire.	There's nothing to do.
42.	J'ai envie de...	I feel like...
43.	J'ai l'intention de...	I plan to...
44.	J'aimerais mieux...	I'd rather...
45.	La dernière fois	The last time
46.	Au passé	In the past
47.	La prochaine fois	The next time
48.	À l'avenir	In the future
49.	Est-ce que tu es libre? (Est-ce que vous êtes libre?)	Are you doing anything?
50.	Est-ce que tu voudrais aller avec moi au cinéma? (Est-ce que vous voudriez aller avec moi au cinéma?)	Would you like to go with me to the movies?
51.	Malheureusement, je ne peux pas.	Unfortunately, I can't.
52.	Peut-être une autre fois.	Perhaps some other time.
53.	Je n'ai pas le temps.	I don't have the time.
54.	Je n'ai pas l'argent.	I don't have the money.
55.	Je suis occupé(e).	I'm busy.
56.	On y va.	Let's get going.
57.	Allons-y.	
58.	Il faut que j'aille.	I have to get going.
59.	Il faut que je parte.	

60. Au voleur!	Stop, thief!
61. Au feu!	Fire!
62. Au secours!	Help!

LESSON THIRTEEN

I. What to Say

Having Fun

Learning a foreign language doesn't have to be hard work. In fact, one of the best ways to learn is simply to socialize with native speakers of the language. Children learn to speak French quickly if they have the opportunity to play with French-speaking children on the playground. Teenagers and adults learn better if they have the chance to mingle regularly with French speakers at parties or other social events. In general, people seem to learn better when they are having fun.

This lesson presents a number of expressions that children use when playing games and having fun. Some of these expressions might also be used by teenagers and adults for games, role play, and occasionally for conversation.

Fun and Games

When your friends are telling you to hurry up, maybe because they're eager to get to the amusement park, you can tell them:

63. J'arrive!	I'm coming!

Don't forget to add expression *Bleues #30:*

Reste couvert.	Keep your shirt on.

When you get there, remember that you have to take turns:

64. À qui le tour?	Whose turn is it?
65. À moi!	It's my turn!

And if you would like to have a race, you may use the following:

66. Préparez-vous...   Ready...Set...Go!
Partez!

When rooting for someone, you can cheer:

67. Vas-y! Vas-y!   Go! Go!
(Allez-y! Allez-y!)   Get going!

If the race was a tie, you may have to use *Blanches #25* to pick the winner:

Pile ou face.   Heads or tails.

Some games require using slow, deliberate movements:

68. Vas-y doucement.   Take it easy.
(Allez-y doucement).   Easy does it.

69. Ne bouge pas.   Don't move.
(Ne bougez pas.)

70. Ne bouge rien.   Don't move a muscle.
(Ne bougez rien.)

Some indoor games must be played in silence. You can also use this one to get someone to keep a secret:

71. Bouche close!   Mum's the word!

At one time or another, everyone has used the expressions "You're getting warmer" and so on. Here's what you say in French:

72. Tu brûles!   You're getting hot!
(Vous brûlez!)

73. Tu gèles!   You're getting cold!
(Vous gelez!)

74. Oui, c'est ça!   Yes, that's it!

Here are some key expressions for "Cops and Robbers":

75. Haut les mains!   Stick 'em up!

76. Ne tirez pas!   Don't shoot!

77. Le champ est libre.   The coast is clear.

If you're in the mood to play a practical joke, you can suggest:

78. Histoire de rire...   Just for fun...

For example:

Histoire de rire, racontons-lui qu'il y a une araignée (*a spider*) sur sa chemise.

This one you will use only one day a year, but it's a good one:

79. Poisson d'avril!   April fools!

Be Careful!

Frequently before you go out, your mother or father may remind you to be careful:

80. Sois prudent!   Be careful!
(Soyez prudent!)

81. Prends garde!   Beware!
(Prenez garde!)

82. Fais attention!   Pay attention!
(Faites attention!)

For example:

Fais attention en traversant la rue!

If you should hear someone excitedly shout out a warning beginning with **Attention,** quickly get out of the way:

83. Attention à la voiture!   Look out for that car!

If you're playing too rough, you might hear:

84. Tu vas te casser la figure!   You're going to break your neck!

Of course you would probably answer:

85. Ne t'inquiète pas. (Ne vous inquiétez pas.)   Don't worry.

II. Application   A. Select the most appropriate expression for each of the following situations:

    1. You're riding the subway in Montreal with your friend Nicole. You notice that there's an unusually large spider crawling on her shoulder, and you think you can quickly knock it to the floor with a magazine if she holds still. You calmly say:

        a. À qui le tour?

        b. Tu brûles!

        c. Ne bouge rien!

    2. You're at your brother's last soccer game of the year. He hasn't scored a goal all season, and you hope today will be his lucky day. With the score tied and only twenty seconds left in the game, your brother rushes toward the goal with the

ball. To encourage him, you shout the following as loud as you can:

    a. Haut les mains!

    b. Ne tirez pas!

    c. Vas-y! Vas-y!

3. In preparation for an assembly your school is having on Monday, your French Club has spent the entire weekend making an Eiffel Tower out of dominoes on the gym floor. Because the project was your idea, you have the honor of placing the very last piece into position. As you carefully set domino number 10,378 in place, your friend, Gisèle, whispers:

    a. J'arrive.

    b. Vas-y doucement.

    c. Préparez-vous...Partez!

4. You're at the Louvre in Paris with your friend, Didier. Distracted by an unusual painting as you walk through the museum, you almost bump into a sculpture standing in your path. Fortunately, Didier is able to discreetly warn you by saying:

    a. Attention à la sculpture!

    b. Bouche close!

    c. Le champ est libre!

5. It's April 1st and you and your sister decide to play a joke on your mother. First, you put shaving cream on the telephone receiver and then carefully hang up the phone. Next, your sister runs next door and asks your neighbor if she can use their phone to call your house. When the phone rings, your mother answers it and hears:

    a. Tu vas te casser la figure, Maman!

    b. Poisson d'avril!

    c. Tu gèles!

B. Complete the following based on the expressions discussed in this lesson.

1. Haut les mains!

—Ne _____ pas!

2. À qui le _____ ?

—À moi.

3. Oh là là! Regarde la glace sur le trottoir! On glisse partout!

—Sois _____ ! Tu vas te casser la _____ !

4. Gilbert! Vite! Quelque chose d'horrible est arrivé! Dépêche-toi!

—J' _____ . Qu'est-ce qu'il y a?

III. Amusez-vous!   *Locutions Bouleversées*

Below are seven expressions from Lesson 13. The letters in each word have been scrambled, but the words themselves have not. Unscramble each expression and write your answers below:

1. TAHU   ELS   NAMIS

_ _ _ _   _ _ _   _ _ _ _ _

2. NERZPE   DAGER

_ _ _ _ _ _   _ _ _ _ _

3. EL   CPMAH   TES   BELRI

_ _   _ _ _ _ _   _ _ _   _ _ _ _ _

4. YESOZ   DURTEPN

_ _ _ _ _   _ _ _ _ _ _ _

5. SITOHIRE   ED   RERI

_ _ _ _ _ _ _ _   _ _   _ _ _ _

6. HEBUCO   SLOCE

_ _ _ _ _ _   _ _ _ _ _

7. TAFISE   TINOTANTE

_ _ _ _ _ _   _ _ _ _ _ _ _ _ _

IV. Take These with You

63. **J'arrive.**	I'm coming.
64. **À qui le tour?**	Whose turn is it?
65. **À moi!**	It's my turn!
66. **Préparez-vous... Partez!**	Ready...Set...Go!
67. **Vas-y! Vas-y! (Allez-y! Allez-y!)**	Go! Go! Get going!
68. **Vas-y doucement. (Allez-y doucement.)**	Take it easy. Easy does it.
69. **Ne bouge pas. (Ne bougez pas.)**	Don't move.
70. **Ne bouge rien. (Ne bougez rien.)**	Don't move a muscle.
71. **Bouche close!**	Mum's the word!
72. **Tu brûles! (Vous brûlez!)**	You're getting hot!
73. **Tu gèles! (Vous gelez!)**	You're getting cold!
74. **Oui, c'est ça!**	Yes, that's it!
75. **Haut les mains!**	Stick 'em up!
76. **Ne tirez pas!**	Don't shoot!

77. Le champ est libre.	The coast is clear.
78. Histoire de rire...	Just for fun...
79. Poisson d'avril!	April fools!
80. Sois prudent! (Soyez prudent!)	Be careful!
81. Prends garde! (Prenez garde!)	Beware!
82. Fais attention! (Faites attention!)	Pay attention!
83. Attention à la voiture!	Look out for that car!
84. Tu vas te casser la figure!	You're going to break your neck!
85. Ne t'inquiète pas. (Ne vous inquiétez pas.)	Don't worry.

LESSON FOURTEEN   Doing a Good Job

Lesson 14, the final lesson in this book, will outline what to say when working with others and when learning and teaching new skills. Such interaction requires language designed for encouraging others and for expressing the frustration that normally occurs when learning something new.

I. What to Say

Getting Started

What do you say when you have been asked a question and you don't know the answer? Although many people don't like to admit there's something they don't know, it's usually best to be honest and say:

86. Je ne sais pas.	I don't know (how).

Use the infinitive to say that you don't know *how* to do something:

Je ne sais pas nager.	*I don't know how* to swim.
Je ne sais pas danser.	*I don't know how* to dance.
Je ne sais pas faire du ski.	*I don't know how* to ski.

Imagine you have decided to take ski lessons. Your instructor might start out by telling you how easy skiing really is:

87. C'est simple comme bonjour!   It's as easy as 1-2-3!

Your first day on the slopes, after explaining some of the basics of the sport, your instructor would certainly say the following in an effort to get you to relax and to concentrate:

88. Ça ne presse pas.   Take your time. There's no hurry.

When you take your first fall, you'll probably say:

89. Zut!   Darn it!

Your instructor might add:

90. Tant pis.   It can't be helped.

After your second fall, you might worry that you haven't fastened your bindings properly. Your instructor would probably take a look at them and assure you:

91. C'est bien comme ça.   It's just fine the way it is.

If you get upset because you're having trouble getting the hang of it, you might hear these words of encouragement:

Rouges #85:   **Ne t'inquiète pas. (Ne vous inquiétez pas.)**   Don't worry.

92. **Du calme!**	Calm down!
93. **Calme-toi!** (**Calmez-vous!**)	
94. **Courage!**	Cheer up!
95. **Tiens bon.** (**Tenez bon.**)	Never give up.

After your third fall, you might say:

96. **Pitié!**	Have a heart! Give me a break!

Sometimes there are friends watching who can add to your misery. When this happens, the following two expressions can come in handy:

97. **Tais-toi!** (**Taisez-vous!**)	Be quiet!
98. **Va t'en!** (**Allez-vous-en!**)	Get out of here!

If a bad fall leads to further frustration, your instructor might suggest a fresh start:

99. **Il faut recommencer à zéro.**	You have to start from scratch.

After a while, however, you'll certainly get the hang of it, and you'll be given a chance to practice your newly acquired skills. Your instructor will say:

100. **Bon travail.**	Good job.

As you practice your snowplow, your instructor will surely express his approval:

101. **À la bonne heure!**	Good for you! You're doing a great job! Job well done!

102. Va toujours!   Keep it up!
  (Allez toujours!)

Let's hope you won't let it go to your head and be tempted to try your hand at some daring, new maneuver like a double flip with a full twist in pike position. If you do, your instructor might ask:

103. Òu est ta tête?   Where is your head?
  (Où est votre tête?)   What are you thinking of?

Of course, he'll get you back to practicing your snowplow and then he'll say:

104. C'est plutôt comme   That's more like it!
  ça!

You'll probably mutter to yourself:

105. C'est la vie!   That's life!
                                That's the way it goes!

You'll feel great, though, at the end of your lesson when you realize how much you have learned. Before you leave, your instructor will certainly wish you good luck:

106. Bonne chance.   Good luck.

II. Application   A. Select the most appropriate expression for each of the following situations:

1. You are an avid chess player. Your friend Valérie would like you to teach her how to play the game, but she's afraid it might be too difficult. You reassure her it isn't by saying:

    a. Tais-toi.

    b. C'est simple comme bonjour!

    c. C'est la vie!

2. Your rock band is holding practice in your parents' garage. Halfway through one of the numbers, someone hits a sour note and the music stops. Guillaume, who plays keyboard, realizes he played the wrong chord and that if everyone would be patient, he'll be able to correct it. So he won't feel rushed, you remark:

    a. Ça ne presse pas, Guillaume.

    b. Zut! Il faut recommencer à zéro.

    c. Va t'en, Guillaume! Tu ne sais pas jouer du clavier éléctronique.

3. Your sister is working on her art project, which has to be handed in tomorrow. It's a self-portrait, and she's upset because she can't paint the nose right. You honestly think it looks pretty good, so you tell her:

    a. C'est la vie!

    b. Où est ta tête?

    c. C'est bien comme ça.

4. Your math teacher gave your class a particularly challenging problem to solve for homework. She remarked that even the best students in the class will have to spend about an hour on this problem. Your math grades have been slipping, so you would like to hand in the correct answer. After working on the assignment for three hours, you finally figure out the correct answer. The next day, your teacher congratulates you for having turned in the correct answer by saying:

    a. Bonne chance.

    b. Tant pis!

    c. À la bonne heure!

5. You and your friends have spent about an hour building a house out of playing cards. As the last card is being set into position, Chantal opens a window to let in some air. Unfortunately, the draft scatters the cards around the room. Chantal reacts by saying:
   a. Bon travail.
   b. Allez toujours!
   c. Pitié!

B. Complete the following responses based on the expressions discussed in this lesson. Choose your answers from the words in the box given below:

1. Oh là là! J'ai oublié de faire mes devoirs!

   —Où est ta _____ ?

2. Regarde, Maman! Je peux nager!

   —Va _____ !

3. Zut! Nous n'avons pas gagné le match!

   —C'est la _____ .

4. J'ai un examen difficile aujourd'hui.

   —Bonne _____ .

5. Georges, savez-vous qui a écrit *Madame Bovary?*

   —Je ne _____ pas, Monsieur.

tête	sais
chance	vie
toujours	

III. Take These with You

86. Je ne sais pas.	I don't know (how).
87. C'est simple comme bonjour!	It's as easy as 1-2-3!
88. Ça ne presse pas.	There's no hurry. Take your time.
89. Zut!	Darn it!
90. Tant pis.	It can't be helped.
91. C'est bien comme ça.	It's just fine the way it is.
92. Du calme!	Calm down!
93. Calme-toi! (Calmez-vous!)	
94. Courage!	Cheer up!
95. Tiens bon. (Tenez bon).	Never give up!
96. Pitié!	Have a heart! Give me a break!
97. Tais-toi! (Taisez-vous!)	Be quiet.
98. Va t'en! (Allez-vous-en!)	Get out of here!
99. Il faut recommencer à zéro.	You have to start from scratch.
100. Bon travail.	Good job.
101. À la bonne heure!	Good for you! You're doing a great job!
102. Va toujours! (Allez toujours!)	Job well done! Keep it up!

103. **Où est ta tête?**
     (Où est votre tête?)

Where is your head?
What are you thinking of?

104. **C'est plutôt comme ça.**

That's more like it.

105. **C'est la vie!**

That's life!
That's the way it goes!

106. **Bonne chance.**

Good luck.

Part II

....

SITUATIONS: One Liners,
Brief Encounters,
and Conversations

▼

SITUATIONS:

One Liners, Brief Encounters, and Conversations

Now that you have familiarized yourself with all the expressions in *Au courant,* you are invited to practice using them in everyday situations. Here's how the Situations in Part II work:

1. You will be given a situation in English and a statement or question in French to which you must respond using the expressions from *Au courant.*

2. You will also be directed to a specific set of expressions from which you can draw your answer. You pick the expression that you feel is the most appropriate for that particular situation.

3. A follow-up sentence in French will be provided to help you respond.

4. It is important for you to understand that *not all the expressions in the set are appropriate for the situation,* so be prepared to justify the expressions you choose.

Here's an example:

SITUATION You're standing in the lunch line and your friend Marie sneezes.

YOU HEAR: **Atchoum!**

YOU SAY: _____

(Bleues #9–14)

Est-ce que tu as besoin d'un mouchoir, Marie?

Look at the *Locutions bleues* #9 through #14 in the Appendix and decide which of the five expressions is the best response in this particular situation. In your opinion, is the best answer **À tes souhaits** (or **À vos souhaits**)? If it is, write your answer on the line provided.

As in real life, there can often be more than one response to a given question. Any expression appropriate for the situation is acceptable as long as it is taken from the set of *Locutions bleues* #9 through #14. Therefore, expressions #9, #10, and #13 are also possible answers, but #11 and #14 probably would not be acceptable. Don't forget to use the lists of *Locutions* provided in the Appendix.

One-Liners

1. SITUATION   You're waiting for a bus in Paris. A lady approaches and asks you a question. You can't understand what she is asking because of the noise from a nearby construction site.

YOU HEAR: Mons**ur, à que*** ***re est-ce q** l'aut**** arri***?

YOU SAY: _____

(Blanches #7–14)

Je ne peux pas vous entendre!

2. SITUATION   You accidentally bump into your friend Denise in the school cafeteria, knocking her tray right out of her hands. She tried to warn you, but it was too late.

YOU HEAR: Attention Nicole!

YOU SAY: _____

(Bleues #9–13)

C'est de ma faute, Denise.

3. SITUATION   For fun, your little brother Mike likes to climb the trees in front of your house. You look out the front window and notice he has climbed much too high and is crying because he can't get down.

YOU HEAR: Au secours! Au secours!

YOU SAY: _____

(Rouges #64–70)

Je vais aller chercher l'échelle tout de suite, Michel! Je t'aiderai.

4. SITUATION Your friend Dan wants you to go with him to a soccer game Sunday afternoon. Unfortunately you can't go because you have to work on a big science project that is due Monday.

YOU HEAR: Frank, est-ce que tu voudrais aller avec moi au match de football dimanche après-midi?

YOU SAY: _____

(Rouges #51–58)

J'ai trop de devoirs dimanche. Peut-être une autre fois. Merci.

5. SITUATION You call your friend Cathy to tell her the big news: You've decided to run for president of the student council. Cathy's mother answers the phone and tells you that Cathy is not home at the moment but is expected back very soon.

YOU HEAR: J'en suis désolée, Paul, mais Catherine n'est pas là...mais je crois qu'elle reviendra bientôt. Est-ce que tu voudrais laisser un message?

YOU SAY: Merci Madame, mais _____

(Blanches #87–90)

Au revoir, Madame.

6. SITUATION You're having trouble with your math homework because it's too noisy in the house and you can't concentrate. Just when things seem to be quieting down, the doorbell rings. Your sister answers the door and invites several people in. They happen to be members of your sister's rock group, and they're looking for a place to practice.

YOU HEAR: Oui...Bien entendu...Nous pouvons jouer dans la salle de séjour. Entrez tout le monde. Allons-y!!!

YOU SAY: _____

(Bleues #39–45)

Je vais à la bibliothèque!

7. **SITUATION**   You are approached by a man who asks you in French if the Rivoli Theater is nearby. Since it isn't within walking distance you suggest he take a cab.

YOU HEAR: Pardonnez-moi, Monsieur. Est-ce que le Théâtre Rivoli est près d'ici? Est-ce que je peux y aller à pied?

YOU SAY: _____

(Blanches #76–79)

Le Théâtre Rivoli est trop loin...à l'autre côté de la ville.

8. **SITUATION**   Your family is trying to decide where to go on vacation this summer. Your dad wants to take the family fishing in the mountains. Your mother, who knows that everyone else in the family would prefer to go to the seashore, informs him that the mountains may not be such a good idea. You agree with your mom.

YOU HEAR: Oh là là! La pêche encore! Qui voudrait aller à la pêche? Personne. Louis, on aimerait mieux aller à la plage cet été. À vrai dire, je ne veux pas encore aller à la pêche cet été.

YOU SAY: _____

(Rouges #23–30)

Je préfère aller à la plage aussi, Papa.

9. **SITUATION**   You have a friend who blames everyone for his problems but himself. Today he received a failing grade on a biology test, but he refuses to admit that it's because he didn't study. You tell him the truth.

YOU HEAR: Ce prof de biologie est fou! Regarde la note qu'il m'a donnée! Qu'est-ce que je vais faire? Le prof ne m'aime pas!

YOU SAY: _____

(Bleues #29–36)

Le prof t'aime, mais tu n'étudies jamais la biologie. Étudie et tu réussiras!

10. **SITUATION**   A good friend recently borrowed ten dollars from you to buy a present for her mother. After about a week, she would like to pay you back, but she still doesn't have the money. You reassure her that there isn't any hurry and that she can pay you back whenever she can.

YOU HEAR: J'en suis désolée, Denise, mais je n'ai pas encore l'argent que tu m'as prêté la semaine dernière.

YOU SAY: _____

(Rouges #85–90)

Je n'ai pas besoin de l'argent maintenant.

Brief Encounters

1. SITUATION   You're visiting Sacré-Cœur in Paris with your friend Jacques. A street vendor approaches you and asks you if you'd like to buy one of the souvenirs he is selling. Shocked that it's so expensive, you tell him that you're just not interested.

YOU HEAR: Monsieur...Monsieur...Voulez-vous acheter une belle Tour Eiffel en plastique? Trente francs la pièce!

YOU SAY: Trente francs la pièce...

_____

(Bleues #1–4)

Incroyable! N'est-ce pas, Jacques? Trente francs pour une Tour Eiffel en plastique!

HE REACTS: Pardonnez-moi, Monsieur...J'ai dit treize francs la pièce! Voulez-vous l'acheter?

YOU ANSWER: _____

(Rouges #33–39)

Je n'en ai pas besoin. Merci.

2. SITUATION   You're shopping at the mall, and you run into your friend Kelly and her cousin Yvette. Yvette is from Montreal, and she's planning to spend the summer in town. After introducing you to Yvette, Kelly invites you to go with them to see a movie after they finish their shopping, and you accept.

YOU HEAR: Marie! Ici Marie! Viens ici! Je voudrais te présenter à ma cousine Yvette de Montréal.

YOU SAY: _____

(Rouges #6–8)

Et Kelly...Ça marche?

KELLY SAYS: Ça marche bien, merci. Nous voulons aller au cinéma ce soir. Est-ce que tu voudrais aller avec nous?

YOU REACT: _____

(Bleues #1–4)

Quel film avez-vous l'intention de voir?

3. SITUATION Your best friend, Sylvie, excitedly informs you that she saw your boyfriend with another girl Friday night. You don't believe her because your boyfriend said he was sick Friday night.

SYLVIE SAYS: J'en suis désolée, Monique...mais j'ai quelque chose d'important à raconter ...J'ai vu Pierre avec Natalie vendredi soir à la bibliothèque.

YOU SAY: _____

(Blanches #7–14)

Qu'est-ce qui y a?

SYLVIE SAYS: J'ai dit que j'ai vu Pierre avec Natalie vendredi soir.

YOU SAY: _____

(Bleues #34–38)

Ce n'est pas vrai parce que Pierre m'a dit qu'il était malade vendredi soir.

4. SITUATION You're in Paris and you've been invited by a friend to have dinner at his house. You decide it would be a nice gesture to buy flowers for his mother. You enter a florist shop and purchase some daisies.

FLORIST: Vous désirez, Monsieur?

YOU SAY: Je voudrais ces marguerites-ci, s'il vous plaît... _____

_____

(Blanches #27–31)

FLORIST: Vingt-cinq francs la douzaine.

YOU SAY: _____

(Blanches #32–#35)

5. **SITUATION**   Your mother tells you the bad news: Mr. Martin, your next-door neighbor, died during the night. At first you can't believe it, then you ask how it happened.

YOUR MOM: Je viens d'entendre que M. Martin est mort pendant la nuit.

YOU SAY: _____

(Blanches #7–14)

Qu'est-ce qui est arrivé?

YOUR MOM: Il a eu une crise cardiaque.

YOU SAY: _____

(Bleues #14–19)

Et il était si jeune! Quel désastre!

Conversations

1. **SITUATION**   Your mother has just won fifteen million dollars in the state lottery, and your parents have decided to surprise you with a brand-new sports car. At first you think she's joking, but then you realize that it's really true.

YOUR MOM: David! Voici ta nouvelle voiture de sport! Viens...Regarde dans le garage!

YOU: _____

(Bleues #14–19)

La seule chose dans le garage qui m'appartient est mon vélo!

YOUR MOM: Mais non, David. Tu ne comprends pas. C'est vrai! Je ne blague pas. J'ai gagné le loto ce matin et nous t'avons acheté une voiture de sport.

YOU: _____

(Rouges #23–26)

Si tu veux. Tu as gagné le loto, et moi, j'ai une réunion avec François Mitterrand ce soir.

(You follow your parents out to the garage.)

YOUR MOM: Et voilà! Ta nouvelle voiture de sport italienne!

YOU: Oh là là! _____
(Bleues #1–4)

C'est vrai? Maman a gagné le loto?

YOUR DAD: Incroyable, n'est-ce pas? Tu l'aimes?

YOU: C'est super! _____
(Rouges #9–13)

Allons-y! Faisons une promenade!

YOUR MOM: D'accord, David. Mais n'oublie pas...Il faut toujours obéir le code de la route.

YOU: _____
(Rouges #9–13)

Je serai prudent. En route!

2. SITUATION It's late Saturday morning and you're sleeping in. Your little brother comes into your room to wake you up and begins to ask you personal questions about the date you had last night.

YOUR BROTHER: Réveille-toi, Robert! Il est 11h 30. Lève-toi!

YOU: _____
(Bleues #5–7)

Laisse-moi dormir.

YOUR BROTHER: À quelle heure es-tu rentré hier soir?

YOU: _____
(Bleues #37–40)

Maintenant va t'en!

YOUR BROTHER: Je sais que tu es rentré après minuit hier soir. Papa et Maman étaient furieux.

YOU: _____

(Bleues #41–46)

Va t'en. Vite!

YOUR BROTHER: À propos, ton prof de mathématiques a téléphoné à Papa hier soir. Tu ne fais pas attention en classe, n'est-ce pas? Pourquoi est-ce que tu n'es pas sage à l'école comme moi?

YOU: _____

(Bleues #14–19)

Tu poses trop de questions, tu sais, Henri.

YOUR BROTHER: Il y a eu un autre coup de téléphone pour toi aussi...une jeune fille qui dit qu'elle est dans ta classe de français. Est-ce que tu voudrais savoir son nom?

YOU: _____

(Bleues #20–24)

Henri?...Henri?...Reviens Henri! Henri, où vas-tu?

3. SITUATION There's a message for you on your answering machine from your French friend Monique, who lives in Lyon. She says she has some big news and that she will call back later to tell you all about it. You can't wait until then, so you call her back immediately.

MONIQUE'S MOTHER: Allô.

YOU: _____

(Blanches #15–19)

Est-ce qu'elle est là?

MONIQUE'S MOTHER: Qui est à l'appareil?

YOU: _____

(Blanches #82–86)

Monique m'a téléphoné cet après-midi et je me demande...

MONIQUE: Salut! Est-ce toi? Comment ça va?

YOU: Salut, Monique _____

_____

(Bleues #5–8)

Tu as dit que tu as une grande nouvelle.

MONIQUE: Oui. D'accord! Grâce à la compagnie de mon père, toute la famille va déménager aux États-Unis... et nous allons habiter à San Diego, la même ville que toi! Formidable, n'est-ce pas?

YOU: _____
(Bleues #14–19)

Mais quand arriverez-vous à San Diego?

MONIQUE: Le 9 juillet. Oh, zut!... Il faut que je parte maintenant. Je t'écrirai une lettre avec tous les détails. Au revoir.

YOU: _____
(Rouges #17–22)

Bonne chance, Monique.

4. SITUATION You're spending a week visiting your cousins Thérèse and Mathieu, who live in Ottawa, Ontario. Together, you're enjoying a sunny but cold Sunday afternoon skating on the Rideau Canal. In spite of the crowd, Mathieu feels like having a race.

MATHIEU: Est-ce que tu voudrais faire une course avec moi?

YOU: _____
(Rouges #9–13)

Et certainement, je vais gagner.

MATHIEU: Tu blagues! Notre grand-mère peut patiner plus vite que toi!

YOU: _____
(Rouges #34–40)

La dernière fois, tu as perdu par trois secondes.

THÉRÈSE: Mathieu, où est ta tête? Il y a trop de monde ici aujourd'hui. Tu vas te casser la figure!

YOU: _____ , Monique.
(Rouges #92–95)

Allons-y, Mathieu. Le champ est libre.

THÉRÈSE: N'importe...mais prenez garde!

YOU: _____
(Rouges #105, 106)

Tu es prêt, Mathieu?

MATHIEU: Et comment!

THÉRÈSE: Préparez-vous...partez!

YOU: _____ , Thérèse!
(Rouges #17–22)

On y va!

5. SITUATION You and your parents are vacationing in France. While in Paris, you decide it would be a great idea to purchase a reasonably priced painting at the Place du Tertre near Sacré-Cœur. Your mother likes a particular painting, but you think it's overpriced (You're paying for it yourself). You decide to buy a different painting.

YOUR MOTHER: Regarde cette toile-là! Qu'en penses-tu? À mon avis, elle est parfaite!

YOU: _____
(Bleues #1–4)

Trois cents francs! Je voudrais quelque chose beaucoup moins cher, Maman.

YOUR FATHER: Mais c'est un beau paysage de...de...la Seine...je crois.

YOU: _____
(Blanches #29, 30)

Je ne veux pas une peinture d'un fleuve dans ma chambre. Regardons ces deux peintures-là, peut-être.

YOUR MOTHER: D'accord. J'aime beaucoup la voiture de sport, mais l'autre...Pouah! Ça ne me plaît pas. Et toi, laquelle est-ce que tu préfères?

YOU: _____

(Bleues #9–12)

Je préfère l'autre.

YOUR FATHER: C'est un peu bizarre...mais si tu veux...

_____

(Blanches #56–60)

Je vais la mettre entre les deux fenêtres.

YOUR MOTHER: À mon avis, la Seine est beaucoup plus belle que cette...cette chose abominable. Mais, vas-y. Ça m'est égal.

YOU: _____

(Blanches #32–35)

Tu es super, Maman!

Part III

APPENDIX: Locutions Bleues, Blanches, and Rouges

APPENDIX:

Locutions Bleues

Lesson 1:
Descriptive Reactions and Responses

1. **Comme c'est beau!**
   Que c'est beau!
   How beautiful it is!
   Boy, is that ever beautiful!

2. **À mon avis, c'est trop cher!**
   In my opinion, it's too expensive!

3. **Quel dommage!**
   What a shame!
   What a pity!

4. **Quelle bonne idée!**
   What a good idea!

Lesson 2:
Expressing Positive Feelings: Concern, Surprise, Enthusiasm, and Joy

5. **Qu'est-ce qui se passe?**
   What's happening?

6. **Qu'est-ce qu'il y a?**
   What's the matter?

7. **Qu'est-ce qui est arrivé?**
   What happened?

8. **Ça te fait mal?**
   (Ça vous fait mal?)
   Does it hurt?

9. **Pauvre petit(e).**
   Pauvre Marie!
   Poor little thing!
   Poor Mary!

10. **J'en suis désolé(e)!**
    I'm sorry!

11. **Mille fois pardon.**
    I'm awfully sorry.

12. À tes souhaits! (À vos souhaits!)	Bless you!
13. Oh là là!	Wow! Oh my goodness!
14. Tu parles! (Vous parlez!)	You've got to be kidding!
15. C'est trop fort!	You're too much!
16. Je n'en reviens pas!	I can't get over it!
17. Tiens, ça c'est nouveau!	Well, that's a new one!
18. Sans blague!	No kidding!
19. Ça tombe bien!	What a coincidence!
20. Félicitations!	Congratulations!
21. Et comment!	You bet! And how!
22. Avec plaisir!	With pleasure!
23. Grâce au ciel!	Thank heavens!
24. Il fait bon vivre!	It's great to be alive!

**Lesson 3:
Expressing Negative
Feelings: Doubt,
Impatience,
Disapproval, and
Anger**

25. Plus ou moins.	More or less.
26. Peut-être.	Maybe. Perhaps.
27. Ça dépend.	That depends.
28. Ça dépend de toi. (Ça dépend de vous.)	That depends on you.

29. **J'en doute!**	I doubt that! I doubt it!
30. **Reste couvert!** **(Restez couvert!)**	Keep your shirt on!
31. **Décide-toi!** **(Décidez-vous!)**	Make up your mind!
32. **N'importe!**	Never mind!
33. **Dépêche-toi!** **(Dépêchez-vous!)**	Hurry up!
34. **Honte à toi!** **(Honte à vous!)**	Shame on you!
35. **J'en ai marre!**	I've had it up to here!
36. **Ras le bol!**	I'm really fed up!
37. **Je m'en fiche!**	I don't give a darn!
38. **Mêle-toi de tes affaires!** **(Mêlez-vous de vos affaires!)**	Mind your own business!
39. **À toi de même!** **(À vous de même!)**	Same to you, buddy!
40. **Bon débarras!**	Good riddance!
41. **Ça, c'est le comble!**	That's the last straw! That beats everything!
42. **Ça me fait rager!**	That burns me up!
43. **Je suis furieux** **(furieuse)!**	I'm furious!
44. **Ça m'inquiète!**	That really bugs me!

45. Assez de bêtises!

Knock it off!
Enough foolishness!

46. Laisse-moi tranquille!
(Laissez-moi
tranquille!)

Leave me alone!

47. Va t'en!
(Allez-vous-en!)

Get out of here!
Go away!

APPENDIX:

Locutions Blanches

Lesson 4:
Expressing Confusion
and Lack of
Understanding

1. **Je t'en prie.**
   (Je vous en prie.)

2. **S'il vous plaît.**

   Please.

3. **Excuse-moi.**
   (Excusez-moi.)

   Excuse me.

4. **Je m'excuse.**

5. **Pardon.**

   Pardon me.

6. **Pardonne-moi.**
   (Pardonnez-moi.)

7. **Je ne comprends pas.**   I don't understand.

8. **Je n'ai pas compris.**   I didn't understand.

9. **Je ne t'ai pas entendu.**   I didn't hear you.
   (Je ne vous ai pas
   entendu.)

10. **Encore une fois.**   Again.
                            One more time.

11. **Répète.**   Repeat.
    (Répétez.)

	12. Parle plus lentement. **(Parlez plus lentement.)**	Speak more slowly.
	13. Est-ce que tu as dit X ou Y? **(Est-ce que vous avez dit X ou Y?)**	Did you say X or Y?
	14. Qu'est-ce que tu as dit? **(Qu'est-ce que vous avez dit?)**	What did you say?
Lesson 5: Expressing Needs, Desires, and Obligations	**15. J'ai besoin d'une serviette!**	
		I need a towel!
	16. Il me faut une serviette!	
	17. Il faut dire <<S'il vous plaît.>>	You must say "Please."
	18. On doit. . .	One should. . .
	19. Je voudrais. . .	I would like. . .
Lesson 6: Going Shopping	**20. Est-ce que je peux vous aider?**	
		May I help you?
	21. Vous désirez?	
	22. Merci, je regarde.	No thanks, I'm only looking.
	23. Lequel (Laquelle) est-ce que tu préfères? **(Lequel [Laquelle] est-ce que vous préférez?)**	Which one do you like better?

24. **Ni l'un(e) ni l'autre.**   Neither one.

25. **Pile ou face.**   Heads or tails.

26. **Je préfère le bleu foncé.**   I prefer the dark blue one.

27. **Est-ce que je peux l'essayer?**   May I try it on?

28. **Comment le trouves-tu? (Comment le trouvez-vous?)**   How do you like it?

29. **Ça me plaît.**   I like it.

30. **Ça ne me plaît pas.**   I don't like it.

31. **Ça coûte combien?**   How much does this cost?

32. **Je le prends. (Je la prends.)**   I'll take it.

33. **Est-ce tout?**   Will that be all?

34. **Comptant ou carte de crédit?**   Cash or charge?

35. **Il n'y a pas de quoi.**   You're welcome.

Lesson 7: Food and Drink

36. **Une table pour deux personnes, s'il vous plaît.**   A table for two, please.

37. **Sur la terrasse, s'il vous plaît.**   On the terrace, please.

38. **Désirez-vous un apéritif?**   Would you like a before-dinner drink?

39. **Rien pour moi, merci.**   Nothing for me, thanks.

40. Je prendrai...	I'll have...
41. Bien cuit	Well done
42. À point	Medium
43. Saignant	Rare
44. Qu'est-ce que vous recommandez?	What do you recommend?
45. Je suis servi(e), merci.	That will be all, thanks.
46. Garçon, l'addition, s'il vous plaît.	Waiter, the check please.
47. Douze francs le kilo!	Twelve francs a kilo!
48. J'ai faim.	I'm hungry.
49. J'ai soif.	I'm thirsty.
50. Je meurs de faim.	I'm dying of hunger.
51. Je meurs de soif.	I'm dying of thirst.
52. J'ai une faim de loup!	I'm so hungry I could eat a horse! (literally: I'm as hungry as a wolf.)
53. À table!	Time to eat!
54. Bon appétit!	Eat hearty! Enjoy!
55. Sers-toi! (Servez-vous!)	Help yourself!
56. Pouah!	Yuk!
57. Un peu	A little bit
58. Un petit peu	A very little bit

	59. **Ça suffit!**	That's enough!
	60. **C'est si bon!**	This is really good!
Lesson 8: **Giving and** **Understanding** **Directions**	61. **Je me suis perdu(e).**	I'm lost.
	62. **Peux-tu me dire comment aller à l'hôpital?** **(Pouvez-vous me dire comment aller à l'hôpital?)**	Can you tell me how to get to the hospital?
	63. **Est-ce que l'hôpital est près d'ici?**	Is the hospital nearby?
	64. **Où se trouve l'hôpital?**	Where is the hospital?
	65. **C'est loin d'ici.**	It's far away.
	66. **C'est tout près.**	It's nearby. It isn't far at all.
	67. **Par ici.**	This way.
	68. **Par là.**	That way.
	69. **Va tout droit.** **(Allez tout droit.)**	Go straight ahead.
	70. **Tourne à droite.** **(Tournez à droite.)**	Turn right.
	71. **Tourne à gauche.** **(Tournez à gauche.)**	Turn left.
	72. **Au feu**	At the light
	73. **Continue.** **(Continuez.)**	Keep going. Continue.

	74. Prends la première rue... **(Prenez la première rue...)**	Take the first street...
	75. Arrête! **(Arrêtez!)**	Stop!
	76. Le (la) voilà!	There it is!
	77. Suis-moi. **(Suivez-moi.)**	Follow me.
	78. Il vaudrait mieux prendre un taxi (le métro).	You're better off taking a taxi (the subway).
	79. Voilà...pour vous.	Here's a little something for you.
Lesson 9: Talking on the Telephone	**80. Allô.**	Hello.
	81. Qui est à l'appareil?	Who is it?
	82. Ici Pierre.	This is Pierre.
	83. Est-ce qu'il (elle) est là?	Is he (she) in?
	84. Ne quitte pas. **(Ne quittez pas.)**	Hang on.
	85. Il (Elle) n'est pas là.	He (She's) not in.
	86. Veux-tu laisser un message? **(Voulez-vous laisser un message?)**	Do you want to leave a message?
	87. Je vais rappeler plus tard.	I'll call back later.

88. **Quand sera-t-il (elle) de retour?**   When will he (she) be back?

89. **Pardon, je ne peux pas t'entendre (vous entendre).**   I'm sorry, I can't hear you.

90. **Un peu plus fort, s'il vous plaît.**   A little louder, please.

91. **La télé, moins fort!**   Turn down the TV!

92. **Tu disais...? (Vous disiez...?)**   You were saying...?

93. **Ce n'est pas urgent.**   It's not important.

94. **Va...je t'écoute. (Allez...je vous écoute.)**   Go on...I'm listening.

95. **Il faut que je raccroche.**   I have to hang up.

96. **Rappelle-moi tout de suite. (Rappelez-moi tout de suite.)**   Call me back right away.

APPENDIX:

Locutions Rouges

Lesson 10:
Making Friends

1. Bonsoir.	Good evening.
2. Salut!	Hi!
3. Ça marche?	How's it going?
4. Quoi de neuf?	What's new?
5. Je te présente mon ami Jean. **(Je vous présente mon amie Jeanne.)**	I'd like you to meet my friend Jean. (I'd like you to meet my friend Jeanne.)
6. Très heureux (heureuse) de faire votre connaissance.	I'm very happy to meet you.
7. Enchanté(e).	Pleased to meet you.
8. Bienvenu(e).	Welcome.
9. Tu danses?	Do you want to dance?
10. Pourquoi pas?	Why not?
11. Merci beaucoup.	Thank you very much.
12. Merci mille fois.	Thanks a million. (literally:

13. Il n'y a pas de quoi.	
14. Pas de quoi.	You're welcome.
15. De rien.	
16. Puis-je?	May I? Can I?
17. À bientôt.	See you soon.
18. À demain.	See you tomorrow.
19. À tout à l'heure.	See you later.
20. Bon voyage!	Have a nice trip!
21. Bonne nuit.	Good night.
22. Fais de beaux rêves! (Faites de beaux rêves!)	Sweet dreams!

Lesson 11: Saying Yes, No, and Maybe

23. D'accord.	OK. I agree.
24. Bien entendu.	Of course.
25. Volontiers!	Gladly!
26. Il n'y a pas d'erreur.	There's no doubt about it.
27. Compte sur moi. (Comptez sur moi.)	You can count on me.
28. Moi aussi.	Me too. So do I.
29. Ni moi non plus.	Neither do I.
30. Si.	Yes (when contradicting a negative question).

31. **Ce n'est pas la peine!**	It isn't worth the trouble.
32. **Ce n'est pas ton affaire!**	It's none of your business!
33. **Je ne suis pas né(e) d'hier!**	I wasn't born yesterday!
34. **Jamais de la vie!**	Out of the question!
35. **Tu peux toujours courir!** **(Vous pouvez toujours courir!)**	You can take a flying leap!
36. **Au contraire**	On the contrary
37. **Par contre**	On the other hand
38. **Je pense que oui.** **Je pense que non.**	I think so. I don't think so.
39. **Je crois que oui.** **Je crois que non.**	I believe so. I don't believe so.
40. **J'espère que oui.** **J'espère que non.**	I hope so. I hope not.

Lesson 12: Making Plans

41. **Il n'y a rien à faire.**	There's nothing to do.
42. **J'ai envie de...**	I feel like...
43. **J'ai l'intention de...**	I plan to...
44. **J'aimerais mieux...**	I'd rather...
45. **La dernière fois**	The last time
46. **Au passé**	In the past
47. **La prochaine fois**	The next time

48. **À l'avenir**	In the future
49. **Est-ce que tu es libre? (Est-ce que vous êtes libre?)**	Are you doing anything?
50. **Est-ce que tu voudrais aller avec moi au cinéma? (Est-ce que vous voudriez aller avec moi au cinéma?)**	Would you like to go with me to the movies?
51. **Malheureusement, je ne peux pas.**	Unfortunately, I can't.
52. **Peut-être une autre fois.**	Perhaps some other time.
53. **Je n'ai pas le temps.**	I don't have the time.
54. **Je n'ai pas l'argent.**	I don't have the money.
55. **Je suis occupé(e).**	I'm busy.
56. **On y va.**	Let's get going.
57. **Allons-y.**	Let's be on our way!
58. **Il faut que j'aille.**	
59. **Il faut que je parte.**	I have to get going.
60. **Au voleur!**	Stop, thief!
61. **Au feu!**	Fire!
62. **Au secours!**	Help!

Lesson 13: Having Fun	63. **J'arrive!**	I'm coming!
	64. **À qui le tour?**	Whose turn is it?

65. **À moi!**	It's my turn!
66. **Préparez-vous...** **Partez!**	Ready...Set...Go!
67. **Vas-y! Vas-y!** **(Allez-y! Allez-y!)**	Go! Go! Get going!
68. **Vas-y doucement.** **(Allez-y doucement.)**	Take it easy. Easy does it.
69. **Ne bouge pas.** **(Ne bougez pas.)**	Don't move.
70. **Ne bouge rien.** **(Ne bougez rien.)**	Don't move a muscle.
71. **Bouche close!**	Mum's the word!
72. **Tu brûles!** **(Vous brûlez!)**	You're getting hot!
73. **Tu gèles!** **(Vous gelez!)**	You're getting cold!
74. **Oui, c'est ça!**	Yes, that's it!
75. **Haut les mains!**	Stick 'em up!
76. **Ne tirez pas!**	Don't shoot!
77. **Le champ est libre.**	The coast is clear.
78. **Histoire de rire...**	Just for fun...
79. **Poisson d'avril!**	April fools!
80. **Sois prudent!** **(Soyez prudent!)**	Be careful!
81. **Prends garde!** **(Prenez garde!)**	Beware!
82. **Fais attention!** **(Faites attention!)**	Pay attention!

	83. **Attention à la voiture!**	Look out for that car!
	84. **Tu vas te casser la figure!**	You're going to break your neck!
	85. **Ne t'inquiète pas. (Ne vous inquiétez pas.)**	Don't worry.
Lesson 14: Doing a Good Job	86. **Je ne sais pas.**	I don't know (how).
	87. **C'est simple comme bonjour!**	It's as easy as 1-2-3!
	88. **Ça ne presse pas.**	There's no hurry. Take your time.
	89. **Zut!**	Darn it!
	90. **Tant pis.**	It can't be helped.
	91. **C'est bien comme ça.**	It's just fine the way it is.
	92. **Du calme.**	
	93. **Calme-toi! (Calmez-vous!)**	Calm down.
	94. **Courage!**	Cheer up!
	95. **Tiens bon! (Tenez bon!)**	Never give up!
	96. **Pitié!**	Have a heart! Give me a break!
	97. **Tais-toi. (Taisez-vous!)**	Be quiet!
	98. **Va t'en! (Allez-vous-en!)**	Get out of here!
	99. **Il faut recommencer à zéro.**	You have to start from scratch.

100. Bon travail.	Good job.
101. À la bonne heure!	Good for you! You're doing a great job! Job well done!
102. Va toujours! **(Allez toujours!)**	Keep it up!
103. Où est ta tête? **(Où est votre tête?)**	Where is your head? What are you thinking of?
104. C'est plutôt comme **ça.**	That's more like it.
105. C'est la vie!	That's life! That's the way it goes!
106. Bonne chance.	Good luck.

NTC FRENCH TEXTS AND MATERIAL

Computer Software
French Basic Vocabulary Builder
 on Computer

**Videocassette, Activity Book,
 and Instructor's Manual**
VidéoPasseport—Français

Conversation Books
Conversational French
A vous de parler
Tour du monde francophone Series
 Visages du Québec
 Images d'Haïti
 Promenade dans Paris
 Zigzags en France
Getting Started in French
Parlons français

Puzzle and Word Game Books
Easy French Crossword Puzzles
Easy French Word Games
Easy French Grammar Puzzles
Easy French Vocabulary Games

Humor in French and English
French à la cartoon

**Text/Audiocassette Learning
 Packages**
Just Listen 'n Learn French
Just Listen 'n Learn French Plus
Sans Frontières 1, 2, 3
Practice & Improve Your French
Practice & Improve Your French Plus
How to Pronounce French Correctly

High-Interest Readers
Suspense en Europe Series
 Mort à Paris
 Crime sur la Côte d'Azur
 Évasion en Suisse
 Aventure à Bordeaux
 Mystère à Amboise
Les Aventures canadiennes Series
 Poursuite à Québec
 Mystère à Toronto
 Danger dans les Rocheuses
Monsieur Maurice Mystery Series
 L'affaire du cadavre vivant
 L'affaire des tableaux volés
 L'affaire des trois coupables
 L'affaire québécoise
 L'affaire de la Comtesse enragée

Les Aventures de Pierre et de
 Bernard Series
 Le collier africain
 Le crâne volé
 Les contrebandiers
 Le trésor des pirates
 Le Grand Prix
 Les assassins du Nord

Graded Readers
Petits contes sympathiques
Contes sympathiques

Adventure Stories
Les aventures de Michel et de Julien
Le trident de Neptune
L'araignée
La vallée propre
La drôle d'équipe Series
 La drôle d'équipe
 Les pique-niqueurs
 L'invasion de la Normandie
 Joyeux Noël
Uncle Charles Series
 Allons à Paris!
 Allons en Bretagne!

Intermediate Workbooks
Écrivons mieux!
French Verb Drills

Print Media Reader
En direct de la France

Duplicating Masters
The French Newspaper
The Magazine in French
French Verbs and Vocabulary Bingo
 Games
French Grammar Puzzles
French Culture Puzzles
French Word Games for Beginners
French Crossword Puzzles
French Word Games

Transparencies
Everyday Situations in French

Reference Books
French Verbs and Essentials of Grammar
Nice 'n Easy French Grammar
Guide to French Idioms
Guide to Correspondence in French

Bilingual Dictionaries
NTC's New College French and
 English Dictionary
NTC's Dictionary of *Faux Amis*

For further information or a current catalog, write:
National Textbook Company
a division of *NTC Publishing Group*
4255 West Touhy Avenue
Lincolnwood, Illinois 60646-1975 U.S.A.